The Competitive Status of the U.S. Civil Aviation Manufacturing Industry

A Study of the Influences of Technology in Determining International Industrial Competitive Advantage

Prepared by the U.S. Civil Aviation Manufacturing Industry Panel, Committee on Technology and International Economic and Trade Issues

of the Office of the Foreign Secretary, National Academy of Engineering

and the Commission on Engineering and Technical Systems, National Research Council

Frederick Seitz, Chairman
Lowell W. Steele, Rapporteur

NATIONAL ACADEMY PRESS
WASHINGTON, DC 1985

NATIONAL ACADEMY PRESS • 2101 Constitution Avenue, NW • Washington, DC 20418

This project was supported by the National Aeronautics and Space Administration and administered under Master Agreement No. 79-02702 between the National Science Foundation and the National Academy of Sciences.

Library of Congress Catalog Card Number 84-62636

International Standard Book Number 0-309-03399-3

Printed in the United States of America

Participants at Meetings of the
U.S. Civil Aviation Manufacturing Industry Panel,
Committee on Technology and International
Economic and Trade Issues

Panel

FREDERICK SEITZ (Chairman), Past President, National Academy
of Sciences; President Emeritus, The Rockefeller University
WILLIAM J. ABERNATHY, Professor, Harvard University
Graduate School of Business Administration
JOHN S. BLIVEN, Senior Vice-President, Bankers Trust Company
IRVING BLUESTONE, Professor of Labor Studies, Wayne State
University
FREDERICK W. BRADLEY, Senior Vice-President, Citibank, N. A.
W. PERRY CRADDOCK, Manager, Market Development, Bell
Helicopter Textron
HUGH S. CRIM, Vice-President, Market Assessment and Strategy,
Pratt and Whitney Aircraft Company
WOLFGANG H. DEMISCH, Vice-President, Equity Research
Department, The First Boston Corporation
JAMES J. FOODY, Vice-President, Product Development,
Fairchild Industries, Inc.
CHARLES W. GEORGE, Vice-President and General Manager,
Aircraft Equipment Division, General Electric Company
(retired)
DOUGLAS GINSBURG, Professor, Harvard University Law School
COLIN J. GREEN, Vice-President, Planning and Services,
Sikorsky Aircraft
WILLIS M. HAWKINS, Senior Advisor, Lockheed Corporation
PAUL JOHNSTONE, Vice-President of Operations, Eastern
Airlines (retired)
SIDNEY JONES, American Enterprise Institute
JOHN N. KERR, President, JNK Associates, Inc.
RAY MAJERUS, Secretary-Treasurer, International Union, United
Auto Workers
DAVID C. MOWERY, Assistant Professor of Economics and Social
Science, Carnegie-Mellon University

MICHAEL G. NEUBURGER, Vice-President, International
Division, Beech Aircraft Corporation
JOHN NEWHOUSE, Guest Scholar, The Brookings Institution
JAMES BRIAN QUINN, Professor, Amos Tuck School of Business
Administration, Dartmouth College
NATHAN ROSENBERG, Professor, Department of Economics,
Stanford University
ROGER D. SCHAUFELE, Vice-President Engineering, Douglas
Aircraft Company, McDonnell Douglas Corporation
RICHARD S. SHEVELL, Professor, Department of Aeronautics
and Astronautics, Stanford University
MONTGOMERIE C. STEELE, Senior Chief Engineer, Technical
Support, Garrett Turbine Engine Company
JOHN STEINER, Vice-President, Corporate Product Development,
The Boeing Company (retired)
ALAN R. STEPHEN, Vice-President, Operations, Regional
Airlines Association of America
WILLIAM W. WINPISINGER, President, International Association
of Machinists and Aerospace Workers, AFL-CIO

Rapporteur

LOWELL W. STEELE, Consultant-Technology Planning and
Management

Additional Participants

SALLY BATH, Aerospace Trade Specialist, Office of International
Sector Policy, U.S. Department of Commerce
SAMUEL COLWELL, Director, Market Research, Fairchild
Industries, Inc.
ROBERT V. GARVIN, Manager, International Strategic Planning,
Aircraft Engine Business Group, General Electric Company
CHARLES H. IDE, Manager, Engineering Resources, Aircraft
Equipment Division, General Electric Company
JACK L. KERREBROCK, Former Associate Administrator,
Aeronautics and Space Technology, NASA; R.C. Maclaurin
Professor and Head, Department of Aeronautics and
Astronautics, MIT
VIRGINIA LOPEZ, Director, Aerospace Research Center,
Aerospace Industries Association of America
LOUISE MONTLE, Manager, Industry and Technical Policy, The
Boeing Company

LOUIS T. MONTULLI, Senior Policy Analyst, Deputy to the Assistant Director for National Security, Office of Science and Technology Policy, Executive Office of the President

ROBERT NYSMITH, Deputy Director, Office of Aeronautics and Space Technology, National Aeronautics and Space Administration

ROLF PIEKARZ, Senior Policy Analyst, Division of Policy Research and Analysis, Scientific, Technological, and International Affairs, National Science Foundation

W. STEPHEN PIPER, Coordinator, Aerospace Trade Policy, Office of Industrial Trade Policy

ALAN RAPOPORT, Policy Analyst, Division of Policy Research and Analysis, Scientific, Technological, and International Affairs, National Science Foundation

THEODORE W. SCHLIE, Director, Office of Competitive Assessment, U.S. Department of Commerce

ALLEN SKAGGS, Vice-President, Civil Aviation, Aerospace Industries Association of America

JOHN SLOWIK, Vice-President, Citibank, N. A.

JOSEPH SNODGRASS, Director, Aviation Programs, Civil Aviation Division, Aerospace Industries Association of America

EDWARD STIMPSON, President, General Aviation Manufacturers Association

RON SWANDA, Manager, System Operations, General Aviation Manufacturers Association

JOHN WARD, Manager, Rotorcraft Office, Office of Aeronautics and Space Administration, National Aeronautics and Space Administration

GEORGE WHITE, Professor, Graduate School of Business Administration, Harvard University

ROGER L. WINDBLADE, Manager, Subsonic Aircraft Office, Office of Aeronautics and Space Technology, National Aeronautics and Space Administration

Staff

HUGH H. MILLER, Executive Director, Committee on Technology and International Economic and Trade Issues

MARLENE R.B. BEAUDIN, Study Director, Committee on Technology and International Economic and Trade Issues

BERNARD MAGGIN, Project Manager, Committee on Technology and International Economic and Trade Issues

STEPHANIE ZIERVOGEL, Secretary, Committee on Technology and International Economic and Trade Issues

Committee on Technology and International
Economic and Trade Issues (CTIETI)

Chairman

N. BRUCE HANNAY, National Academy of Engineering Foreign
Secretary and Vice-President, Research and Patents,
Bell Laboratories (retired)

Members

WILLIAM J. ABERNATHY, Professor, Harvard University
Graduate School of Business Administration and Chairman,
CTIETI Automobile Panel (deceased)
JACK N. BEHRMAN, Luther Hodges Distinguished Professor of
International Business, University of North Carolina
CHARLES C. EDWARDS, President, Scripps Clinic and Research
Foundation and Chairman, CTIETI Pharmaceutical Panel
W. DENNEY FREESTON, JR., Associate Dean, College of
Engineering, Georgia Institute of Technology and Chairman,
CTIETI Fibers, Textiles, and Apparel Panel
JERRIER A. HADDAD, Vice-President, Technical Personnel
Development, IBM Corporation (retired)
MILTON KATZ, Henry L. Stimson Professor of Law Emeritus,
Harvard University Law School
RALPH LANDAU, Chairman, Listowel Incorporated* and
Vice-President, National Academy of Engineering
JOHN G. LINVILL, Professor, Department of Electrical
Engineering, Stanford University and Chairman, CTIETI
Electronics Panel

---

*Retired Chairman, Halcon-SD Group, Inc.

vi

RAY McCLURE, Program Leader, Precisions Engineering Program, Lawrence Livermore Laboratory and Chairman, CTIETI Machine Tools Panel

BRUCE S. OLD, President, Bruce S. Old Associates, Inc. and Chairman, CTIETI Ferrous Metals Panel

MARKLEY ROBERTS, Economist, AFL-CIO

LOWELL W. STEELE, Consultant-Technology Planning and Management*

MONTE C. THRODAHL, Vice-President, Technology, Monsanto Company

---

*Formerly Staff Executive, Corporate Technology Planning, General Electric Company

Preface

In August 1976 the Committee on Technology and International Economic and Trade Issues examined a number of technological issues and their relationship to the potential entrepreneurial vitality of the U.S. economy. The committee was concerned with:

- Technology and its effect on trade between the United States and other countries of the Organization for Economic Cooperation and Development (OECD);
- Relationships between technological innovation and U.S. productivity and competitiveness in world trade; impacts of technology and trade on U.S. levels of employment;
- Effects of technology transfer on the development of the less-developed countries (LDCs) and the impact of this transfer on U.S. trade with these nations; and
- Trade and technology exports in relation to U.S. national security.

In its 1978 report, Technology, Trade, and the U.S. Economy,* the committee concluded that the state of the nation's competitive position in world trade is a reflection of the health of the domestic economy. The committee stated that, as a consequence, the improvement of our position in international trade depends primarily upon improvement of the domestic economy. The committee further concluded that one of the major factors affecting the health of our domestic economy is the state of industrial innovation. Considerable evidence was presented during the study to indicate that the innovation process in the United States is not as vigorous as it once was. The committee recommended that further work be undertaken to provide a more

---

*Available from the National Academy Press, 2101 Constitution Avenue, N.W., Washington, DC 20418.

ix

detailed examination of the U.S. government policies and practices that may bear on technological innovation.

The first phase of study based on the original recommendations resulted in a series of published monographs that addressed government policies in the following areas:

- The International Technology Transfer Process.*
- The Impact of Regulation on Industrial Innovation.*
- The Impact of Tax and Financial Regulatory Policies on Industrial Innovation.*
- Antitrust, Uncertainty, and Technological Innovation.*

This report on the civil aircraft manufacturing industry is one of seven industry-specific studies, conducted as the second phase of work by this committee. The other panels set up by the committee addressed automobiles, electronics, ferrous metals, machine tools, pharmaceuticals, and fibers, textiles, and apparel. The objectives of these studies were to (1) identify global shifts of industrial technological capacity on a sector-by-sector basis, (2) relate those shifts in international competitive industrial advantage to technological and other factors, and (3) assess further prospects for technological change and industrial development.

As part of these studies, each panel developed (1) a brief historical description of the industry, (2) an assessment of the dynamic changes that have occurred and are anticipated in the next decade, and (3) policy options and scenarios to describe alternative futures for the idustry. The primary charge to the panel was to develop a series of policy options for consideration by public and private policymakers.

The methodology of the studies included a series of panel meetings involving discussion between (1) experts named to the panel, (2) invited experts from outside the panel, and (3) government agency and congressional representatives presenting current governmental views and deliberations.

The drafting work on this report was done by Lowell S. Steele, formerly of General Electric and now a private consultant. Bernard Maggin was responsible for assisting Dr. Steele by providing research and resource assistance as well as assisting in producing drafts of report material, based on the panel deliberations, that were reviewed and critiqued by the panel members at their meetings.

---

*Available from the National Academy of Engineering, 2101 Constitution Ave., N.W., Washington, D.C. 20418.

Contents

The Competitive Status of the U.S. Civil Aviation Manufacturing Industry

Summary

Civil aircraft manufacture is experiencing profound change, created by a combination of domestic and international circumstances. The industry, comprising large commercial transports, rotorcraft, regional transports, business aircraft, and light piston aircraft, holds a unique position in the nation's industrial structure--in its contribution to trade, its coupling with national security, and its symbolism of U.S. technological strength. Consequently, the implications of the change that is occurring are of national importance.

BACKGROUND

Civil aircraft (including engines and parts) are an important component of manufactured durable goods (sales--including exports of military aircraft--of $17 billion in 1982 represent 1.88 percent of all durables) and a major source of employment for skilled production workers, scientists, engineers, and technicians.

Large transports are the dominant element in sales of civil aircraft, and export sales now represent 60 percent of large transport sales. Exports will become even more important, due to the more rapid growth of air transport in foreign countries. These export sales are vital to the economies of scale that help give cost leadership to the United States.

Aircraft manufacture plays a unique role in national security. The teams that could help develop design and production technology for new military aircraft are kept in a state of increased readiness by the requirements of the civil market. The competitions and requirements of the civil market stimulate technological and product advances that contribute to these associated industries. The production base is also available in an emergency surge capacity. This base comprises not only the aircraft companies,

1

but also a massive specialized infrastructure of some 15,000 firms that supply sophisticated components, materials, and equipment.

The U.S. aviation industry has dominated world markets since the end of World War II. This success, of course, was in part a legacy of the technology and production base created for that war. Additional factors include:

• A generally healthy domestic economy that encouraged an aggressive and effective program of technology development, aircraft design, manufacture, service, and operations.

• A continuing productive relationship among government, the airlines, and the manufacturer.

• An aggressive effort on the part of the airlines and aircraft manufacturers to continually improve surface transportation, resulting in significant passenger advantages in trip time, trip cost, and trip safety.

• The resulting rapid growth in domestic and international air transport.

The history of success began to change in the mid-1970s and has altered the outlook for the United States in all classes of aircraft. These changes include the impact of deregulation on domestic air transport, the emergence of foreign competition, internationalization of aircraft manufacture, and growing involvement of foreign governments in the industry.

United States air transport had grown and matured as an industry in which regulation of routes and fares encouraged focus on passenger amenities and political lobbying for routes rather than on competition in fares and efficiency of operations. Service to smaller communities was of lower priority, and experimentation with fares and service to probe customer preferences was virtually nonexistent.

Deregulation of fares and routes in 1978 has led to greatly increased competition for routes, the appearance of many new carriers, and unprecedented competition and diversity in fares and services. Airlines have responded by seeking to protect or improve their share in markets where they were strongest by emphasizing hub-and-spoke feeder systems. Many new commuter airlines have arisen to serve smaller communities. Evaluation of the effects depends on the use made of air transport. Many frequent travelers experience increased inconvenience in point-to-point service, deterioration in service in many instances, and chaotic fares on many routes, but they can also benefit from frequent-traveler bonuses if they are prepared to accept some inconvenience. Travelers can also obtain dramatically lower fares on many routes and in scheduling benefit from lower fares on some flights and new classes of service on some routes. Service to smaller communities is mixed--some have better service with better equipment, others have seen it deteriorate or disappear.

It is clear that competition is creating constant pressure on fares and that strenuous efforts are being made to reduce costs and improve operating efficiency. Furthermore, the change in route strategy is altering the nature of the optimal fleet mix, with increased need for somewhat smaller aircraft. A large global supply of secondhand aircraft is making it easy for new entrants to lease equipment or buy it at bargain prices, and to some extent is acting as a barrier to the purchase of new aircraft.

The change in competitive environment noted above, combined with a severe recession[1], has had a dramatic effect on the financial performance of the airlines in operation at the time of regulation. Most have experienced severe losses, balance sheets have deteriorated, and perhaps most important, forecasting the future has become much more uncertain. This affects projection of future equipment needs, return on investment, and security of the return. Airlines are displaying great variability in their ability to respond. For example, American Airlines can place a large order for planes at the same time that Continental and Braniff are struggling with bankruptcy and Eastern and TWA face severe cost problems. These changes have, not surprisingly, reduced demand for new aircraft. They also affect the future capability of U.S. airlines to serve as launch customers for new aircraft. Thus, the importance of international markets may grow because large foreign carriers may play a more important role in launching new aircraft.

One important effect of deregulation has been to stimulate the growth of regional airlines. This has in turn stimulated interest in specialized aircraft to serve these markets--aircraft that heretofore had not been attractive to U.S. manufacturers. Thus, demand for cost-effective, smaller transport aircraft represents a new opportunity.

It is difficult to predict the eventual equilibrium after the transition to deregulation, but it is likely that a few strong national carriers will emerge. This panel believes it is important that evaluation of the results of deregulation include its effect on the aircraft manufacturers.

Foreign Competition

The European countries have tried repeatedly to create a viable air transport manufacturing industry. In 1970 efforts were rationalized by creating Airbus Industrie to draw on the resources of a number of countries and to develop a coordinated worldwide marketing approach.

The A300 that resulted from this endeavor is a technically proficient aircraft that has begun to achieve market penetration, reaching a peak of 50 percent of orders for wide-bodied transports in 1982. Airbus has made clear its intention to develop a family of aircraft that will cover generally all of the large commercial transport market.

In the United States the situation regarding the manufacture of other classes of aircraft--rotorcraft, regional transports, executive and business aircraft--is perceived to be urgent. The requirements of these types of aircraft are more within the economic and technical capability of smaller countries. Consequently, for reasons of economic growth, improved foreign trade, and even prestige, they have been targeted for production by many countries--e.g., the United Kingdom, France, Italy, Spain, Japan, Brazil, Indonesia, and Israel.

In rotorcraft, the U.S. industry product line is matched in all significant classes and sizes by competitive foreign helicopters. The long practice of developing civil derivatives of military vehicles is no longer practical, due to the specialized demands for military use. U.S. civil helicopter manufacturing must use private capital to compete with financing granted or guaranteed by foreign governments. Imports of helicopters have grown from 14 percent in 1979 to 35 percent in 1982.

Regional transports present a difficult situation for U.S. manufacturers. As noted above, until recently the U.S. commuter market did not attract the development of specialized aircraft to serve it. Other countries did have such requirements and had developed the needed vehicles. With deregulation leading to increased growth in domestic regional airlines, foreign manufacturers are moving to capitalize on this opportunity. U.S. manufacturers face a dilemma: their own product lines are not extensive; the U.S. market is relatively open to competitors while many foreign markets are closed; and foreign manufacturers--typically supported in some form by their governments--are active in the field and frequently have been for many years.

A desire to avoid a U.S. monopoly worldwide has been an important driving force behind the persistent European effort. It is important to recognize that this increase in the strength of foreign competition is not without its benefits for the U.S. consumer. The demands for capital and for technology development are such that not even the United States can support many suppliers of large transports. It would not be in the interest of the U.S. consumer to have only one domestic supplier--a not improbable scenario.

A factor of more immediate benefit to the U.S. economy is the large U.S. content in foreign-manufactured aircraft--even the A300. For example, engines, controls, and a wide variety of specialized materials and components for most foreign-built aircraft are purchased from U.S. suppliers because economies of scale will not justify local manufacture or because local capacities are inadequate. All of these exports, of course, strengthen U.S. trade and provide domestic employment. This circumstance will not persist without aggressive efforts by U.S. manufacturers to maintain leadership because foreign manufacturers continue to seek ways to increase local content; thus the U.S. content is diminishing. Despite the widespread concern over the strength of the U.S. dollar as an impediment to exports, this concern does not appear to be applicable to the export of large transports. Airbus is regarded as certain to compensate for changes in the rate of exchange irrespective of which way it goes. The large U.S. content also exerts a buffering influence. A strong dollar increases the cost of the U.S. content but reduces pressure on European content and vice versa.

Growing Importance of International Markets

The size and dynamism of the domestic air transport industry that fostered U.S. leadership in aircraft began to change--at least relatively--in the 1970s. The U.S. market grew more slowly (5 percent vs. 9 percent worldwide), and U.S. passenger-miles dropped from 57.5 percent of the free world to 40 percent. Although U.S. manufacturers have always excelled at interpreting the needs of foreign customers, they will have to be even more sensitive in the future. Most foreign airlines are government-owned or -supported. Consequently, purchase of aircraft is often a politicized process that essentially requires approval of, if not negotiation with, governments. The developing countries represent the area of most rapid projected growth in air transport, but they also experience the most difficulty in arranging financing. Consequently, U.S. manufacturers face increasing pressure to help finance the purchase of aircraft. This trend will increase their requirements for raising capital, enlarge their financial exposure to risk, and bring them into confrontation with foreign governments that use financing terms and other government-to-government trade factors as a competitive weapon in the marketplace.

Internationalization of Aircraft Manufacture

The manufacture of aircraft and engines is becoming increasingly internationalized. The growing capital requirements, increased risk, and greater technical complexity associated with aircraft manufacture create pressures to form partnerships. Perhaps more important, the desire of many countries to participate in the industry leads them to use access to their domestic markets as a lever to increase their participation in the industry. These arrangements, of course, encourage a two-way flow in technology from which U.S. manufacturers can benefit to some extent.

The formation of such international partnerships is the subject of controversy, and the relative merits are not easily judged. One must balance denial of access to a market against at least partial access, but with the risk that one may be accelerating the development of technical competence by a potential competitor.

The eventual outcome depends largely on maintaining momentum in long-range domestic aeronautical R&D[2] and the incorporation of advanced technology in new designs. The panel believes that a healthy, effective domestic technology development program is the best possible foundation for maintaining competitive leadership.

Financial Performance of the Industry

Manufacture of large commercial transports is a long-term endeavor that involves committing huge amounts of capital in the face of great market uncertainty. Developing a wholly new aircraft requires four to six years and a $4 to $5 billion investment. Even for a successful venture, return of investment will typically require at least 10 to 15 years.

The great market success of U.S. manufacturers and the long record of technological leadership have not led to outstanding financial performance. The aerospace industry (separate data on civil aircraft are not available on a current basis) has a return on sales and on assets below the average for all manufacturing. Anecdotal data on individual aircraft are even more discouraging. At most, 3 out of 22 commercial jet transports introduced worldwide are thought to have been profitable. Thus, with the changes now confronting the industry, management faces a great challenge.

COMPETITIVE ASSESSMENT OF TECHNOLOGY

Translating advanced technology into products suited to the marketplace has been a major factor in the success of U.S. aircraft manufacturers. As competition intensifies, the timing of the introduction and the fit of the product to the customer's need become increasingly important.

Despite decades of technological progress, there are important areas for continued advance that will improve reliability of aircraft and air travel as well as increase fuel efficiency and efficiency in operations. The integrated effects of a variety of advances in aircraft could improve fuel efficiency by as much as 30 to 50 percent--and some studies are even more optimistic. Introduction of advanced turboprops or propfans could provide up to 20 percent additional improvement, and the experimental unducted propfan engine could raise this figure.

Aeronautical technology is conventionally categorized into seven major areas: design techniques, aerodynamics, flight controls, structures, airframe-propulsion integration, avionics, and propulsion.

Design Techniques

High-speed computers make possible the use of sophisticated computational analysis that reduces dependence on empiricism and experiment. This technology is applicable to all classes of aircraft. The United States is thought to have a slight lead over Europe (and probably a larger lead over Japan) at this time. Nevertheless, European efforts are very good, as shown by the aerodynamic efficiency of the A300 and A310. Japanese strength in electronics provided the foundation for Japan to develop greater capability.

Computer-aided design and computer-aided manufacture (CAD/CAM) permits rapid and effective evaluation of many different designs and allows selected designs to flow directly to manufacturing. The combination of these two technologies permits development of more effective designs at lower cost, with fewer errors and less lead time. CAD/CAM was pioneered in the United States but has been adopted rapidly in Europe (Airbus Industrie) and Japan. The hardware and software for CAD/CAM are rapidly diffused throughout the free world, and foreign manufacturers can be expected to stay competitive in this technology.

Aerodynamics

Improved understanding of the laminar-to-turbulent-flow transition and development of methods to delay the transition can lead to improved aerodynamic efficiency for cruise conditions. The United States is thought to be far ahead in boundary layer management, but the United States and Europe are generally comparable in wing design. For example, the Airbus A310 wing incorporates the latest in high-lift systems to provide excellent takeoff and landing performance.

Flight Controls

Active control systems to improve aircraft stability can provide reductions in drag and weight. Active controls to alleviate stress from wind gusts or maneuvering also offer opportunities to reduce weight or alternatively increase wing aspect ratio and thus reduce drag. U.S. manufacturers and Airbus appear to be approximately equal in both of these fields.

Advanced Structures

New high strength-to-weight alloys and new superplastically formed metals offer significant potential for saving weight. The United States and Europe are regarded as on a par in technology, but the U.S. leads in application experience with new alloys. This lead enables us to project longer "economic life" at this stage of application.

Composite materials offer the greatest opportunity in airframe materials. They offer high stiffness and extremely light weight. Long-term benefits could be a 15 to 20 percent reduction in total structural weight, a 7 to 15 percent improvement in fuel efficiency, and a resulting 4 to 8 percent reduction in direct operating cost--the latter is more uncertain because manufacturing costs for composites and future fuel costs are very uncertain.

European R&D efforts are extensive and continue to accelerate. Aerospatiale has an aggressive program for progressive introduction of composite components on the A300 and the A310 as well as on helicopters and smaller aircraft. The A320 will incorporate still more extensive applications. The United States also is active, but the present NASA program calls for a six-year effort to develop design data for fuselages. Given the moderate pace of the current NASA program and the budget pressures it is encountering, the U.S. position in this very important technology could be threatened.

Propulsion Integration

This technology is regarded as relatively mature for conventional turbofans, and the United States and Great Britain are regarded as equal in nacelle design. Propulsion integration becomes crucial for the high-speed turboprops or propfans that are widely regarded as offering great promise for improved efficiency in smaller transport aircraft. The development of advanced propellers and their gearboxes is central to progress in this field. It is known that the European companies are active, and it would appear that the United States and Europe are about on the same trajectory for applying this technology.

Avionics

Advances in microcircuitry will permit the development of the ultrareliable, fault-tolerant electronic systems that are vital to implementation of active flight controls and computer-integrated flight management systems. Estimates of projected resulting improvements in fuel efficiency and weight reduction show considerable spread, but improvement in fuel efficiency could be up to 20 percent and weight reduction as much as 10 percent. Reduction in operating cost is projected to be 5 to 10 percent.

Much of the historical electronics/avionics capability in commercial transports is a by-product of military technology. In military avionics the United States leads the world, and as long as we retain the close coupling between civil and military avionics technology, it is doubtful whether the United States will be overtaken in the broad field of avionics. It is important to note, however, that the Japanese have already developed advanced cockpit-display technology and that they have the development capability and the potentially lower costs to challenge U.S. leadership, given the opportunity.

Propulsion

The principal foreign competitor in jet engines is Rolls Royce, which has near parity in thrust and specific fuel consumption, but lags in thrust-to-weight ratio and turbine temperature. Rolls Royce has mounted an extensive program to overcome its deficiencies in turbine temperature and will likely have achieved parity--at least in application to engines--by the mid-1980s.

Overall, the United States has a lead in propulsion technology, but it is not unassailable. Furthermore, Great Britain has demonstrated a commitment to maintain a viable presence--a position actively encouraged by her European partners.

Facilities

Aeronautical R&D requires massive and expensive facilities for test, experiment, and simulation. U.S. facilities are thought to be the best in the world; however, European facilities are such that effort is not handicapped. At this stage, Japan is seriously handicapped by the lack of such facilities and by the absence of a manufacturing industry to benefit from the technology.

KEY CHALLENGES AND RECOMMENDATIONS

Growing Involvement of Governments in Trade

The growing involvement of governments in both manufacture and sale of aircraft on the one hand and purchase on the other has important implications for competition and trade. The calculation of costs and benefits by governments is based on broader and more diffuse criteria than is possible for a private company: the time periods for judging results and paybacks are longer, and investments can be sustained for longer periods of time without necessarily ever achieving commercial success.

In this context, the several agreements establishing rules for trade in civil aircraft assume great significance, especially regarding subsidies. This issue is especially complex in the case of aircraft because virtually every developed country, including the United States, has a long history of close government-industry relationships. Despite their limitations, negotiations under the terms of previously agreed trade standards are the only generally accepted vehicle for addressing problems of trade policy. The United States has little choice except to pursue them vigorously. Sales of aircraft are particularly difficult to deal with in this framework because purchases tend to be made infrequently, individual orders are large, and obtaining initial orders gives high leverage for follow-on orders.

Three aspects of trade administration warrant attention:

1. Adequacy of resources and political resolve to support monitoring of trade behavior and to support negotiations in specific transactions, when it is called for, are crucial. Recent steps to strengthen U.S. capability are highly commendable, and it is important that they be sustained in the future.

2. Effective government-industry interaction with respect to the smaller transactions characteristic of sales of helicopters and regional aircraft is increasingly important. Neither the government nor the companies involved have had much experience in such relationships, and it is important for them to be developed.

3. A more flexible and timely response is needed for government action to counteract trade arrangements that constitute unfair practices. Options could include temporary measures such as denial of investment tax credit on the non-U.S. labor content of imported aircraft, closer coordination of military development and industrial need, and more aggressive export finance policies. These measures must be invoked with great care because they invite retaliation, typically where other governments feel they have greatest leverage (not necessarily in the same industry), and they also risk escalation into destructive trade wars.

It should be noted that in each of these areas, as well as in subsequent ones in which the panel will advocate strengthening the U.S. posture, the changes will redound to the benefit of many industries--not just aircraft manufacture.

The panel endorses the recent action in the U.S. Department of Commerce to provide focused attention on the aircraft manufacturing industry as well as in other sectors that are significant in foreign trade and to strengthen administrative support for monitoring trading behavior and encouraging compliance with agreements. The panel recommends that the importance of this activity receive sufficiently broad political endorsement to transcend changes in administration.

The panel recommends continuing vigorous efforts by the United States government to bring into the Agreement on Trade in Civil Aircraft those nonsignatory nations currently or prospectively exporting to the United States.

The panel also recommends more vigorous data collection, monitoring, assessment, and enforcement of the GATT agreement by government personnel for all segments of the aircraft industry, not just large commercial transports.

The panel endorses and recommends continued efforts to eliminate all forms of trade-distorting mechanisms so that normal market forces can operate effectively in all international transactions.

The panel recommends that evaluation of tax policy continue to give appropriate weight to maintaining the international competitiveness of U.S. industry.

Export Credit Financing

Agreements on financing have proved somewhat elusive because of the resolve of foreign governments to establish a viable presence in aircraft manufacture. A "standstill" agreement in 1975 set a maximum of 10 years for repayment--a period much shorter than the life of the aircraft, and one that denied the United States the advantage of its strong long-term capital market, but set no minimum interest. A subsequent "commonline" agreement established a minimum interest rate for large transport aircraft.

The Export-Import Bank (Eximbank) currently employs terms and conditions similar to those of other lenders for large aircraft, with one important exception: it imposes a 2 percent application fee that enlarges the "up front" payment. In the case of developing countries--a market of growing importance--Eximbank employs more rigorous criteria to evaluate "a reasonable assurance of repayment" than many foreign competitors face with their financing agencies. Inconsistency in the application of Eximbank policy has made it difficult for foreign customers to plan purchases and financing. Both of these conditions handicap U.S. manufacturers because purchasers have long memories.

The combination of weakened domestic customers, growing reluctance of traditional lenders to provide funds under conventional arrangements, and uncertain financing from Eximbank has forced aircraft manufacturers to invent new forms of financing. Creative extensions of operating-lease arrangements (leveraged leasing), which make provision for buy-back coupled with transfer of the investment tax credit (ITC) to the lessor, point the way to the trend of the future. U.S. manufacturers have demonstrated ingenuity and a willingness to take risks that are commendable. This emerging trend does increase their financial exposure and reflects a need for still further development of financial instruments (and even new institutions) that can spread risk adequately.

The growing importance of foreign markets means that restrictions on investment tax credit to foreign operators could have a detrimental effect on U.S. aircraft manufacturers.

The panel recommends consideration of additional measures that would enable aircraft manufacturers to spread the risk in leasing aircraft to domestic and foreign customers.

The panel recommends that Eximbank reexamine its mode of operation and lending roles in the light of the heightened international competition facing all of U.S. industry. This report suggests several specific areas warranting attention to ensure that Eximbank is consistent, effective, and responsive to competitive realities.

Smaller Aircraft

Since smaller aircraft are typically sold to customers with very limited capability to finance purchases, financial terms can be a powerful competitive weapon. This weapon is being used aggressively by foreign competitors.

It is important for Eximbank to review its procedures for their appropriateness in the light of the heightened competition U.S. manufacturers are facing. Equally important, Eximbank should seek consistency in its approach and its priorities so that U.S. companies can propose financing terms with greater confidence.

The panel endorses and recommends continuation of the recent new Eximbank facility to provide medium-term loans for sales of small aircraft.

International Trade, Technology Transfer, National Security, and Diplomacy

Trade, technology transfer as part of trade, and national security interests interact in complex ways that affect the U.S. economy and its position in the international marketplace. Control of the export of technology in the interest of national security is unquestionably a legitimate responsibility of the government. The task requires balancing national security or foreign policy objectives with those of strengthening the U.S. economy and preserving the U.S. position in advanced technology.

The balancing process inevitably creates apparent inconsistencies and indecisiveness that are in themselves detrimental to trade because they tend to cast a shadow over the reliability of U.S. manufacturers as sources of supply.

In policy deliberations it is important for realistic attention to be given to assessing the true effectiveness of any proposed restraints, the availability of alternatives, the potential near- and long-term damage to U.S. firms and to the economy, and the opportunities for retaliatory action by the countries being targeted.

National security and foreign policy have powerful advocates within the government. Commercial interests are less easily represented because they are diffuse and not well articulated. Furthermore, in the sphere of international trade it is apparent that the U.S. government places a higher priority on national security versus commerce than do the governments of our trading competitors.

Licensing and coproduction have been important elements of mutual security arrangements for many years. These agreements heighten the sense of partnership, broaden the defense industrial base, and reduce drain on local currencies. NATO allies have insisted on broadening the base of these agreements, and they have no doubt become a vehicle for transfer of both production and design technology. The Memoranda of Understanding (MOU) under which these exchanges occur seek a balancing quid pro quo, but the subject matter may be far afield from commerce. Industry spokesmen have felt that MOUs are negotiated with insufficient input from industry. The U.S. Department of Defense (DOD) is perceived as being very sensitive to possible loss of critical technology through commercial channels, but much less concerned over the possible adverse commercial implications of military agreements for coproduction.

The panel believes it is important for policy deliberations in this area to reflect the changing circumstances of the United States in balancing security and trade, i.e., allies are much stronger economically and represent a growing competitive threat, the technological positions are much closer to parity, international markets are increasingly important to U.S. manufacturers, and aircraft manufacture itself is becoming increasingly internationalized.

In the light of these complexities, the panel recommends that mechanisms be developed that will ensure an effective industrial input to the deliberations on coproduction agreements and that due weight be given to the change in competitive status and relative technological position of U.S. industry in reaching decisions.

Achieving Synergy Between National Security and Civil Aviation

The valuable coupling between national defense and civil aircraft manufacture was noted earlier. Despite the differing requirements for civil and military aircraft, much of the technology base, much of the supplier base, and many of the skills and processes used are common. Historically, civil aircraft have benefited from military technological advances in both airframes and propulsion. Increasingly, a reverse flow has been important, e.g., improved fuel efficiency, flight management systems, and composite structures.

DOD is now supporting the launch of far fewer aircraft. Traditionally, DOD has focused its attention on combat aircraft and has used off-the-shelf technology for support aircraft. There is at present no policy or mechanism for integrating military needs and potential civil programs in cases where mutual benefit would result, e.g., advanced structures, understanding and controlling behavior and use of materials, and new manufacturing techniques.

A related benefit could result from better management of the timing of procurement. The recurring "wild" fluctuations magnify problems of employment instability and, even more, of preserving the key development and production teams on which the entire infrastructure rests. The panel recognizes the practical difficulties in achieving the goal of a mix of civil and military aircraft procurement that would smooth employment. However, in the emerging competitive climate this goal assumes greater urgency. It should be noted that foreign governments commonly encourage development and production of domestic civil aircraft through government-directed purchases of these aircraft by the domestic military establishment.

The panel recommends that DOD, the National Aeronautics and Space Administration (NASA), and the FAA reexamine the mechanisms for working with the civil aircraft manufacturers to ensure that maximum advantage is taken of opportunities for dual-use capabilities in technology development for design, manufacture, and certification.

The panel recommends that DOD and industry seek to strengthen coordinated planning for aircraft procurement so as to reduce, as far as practicable, the great cyclicality in production that disrupts the industry.

Maintaining Momentum in R&D

The bedrock of U.S. leadership in civil aircraft is technology-- its development and incorporation into new designs. That leadership need not be threatened provided that the U.S. maintains a vigorous program of research and development. The National Aeronautics and Space Administration (NASA) is the focal point of aeronautical R&D for both civil and military applications. The high cost of R&D and the massive facilities required for aeronautical R&D preclude any private enterprise from performing NASA's central role.

It is apparent that the space programs dominate the NASA effort--aeronautical R&D represents approximately 5 percent of NASA's total R&D budget. It is difficult to compare directly the effort of the United States with the aggregate of its competitors; however, they are approximately equal for generic R&D. In addition, however, in Europe and elsewhere specific competing products are also developed with public funds, and the technical performance of the equipment indicates that it rests on a solid base of technology. The panel questions the present priorities of NASA resource allocations--given the economic and social importance of civil aviation and the altered competitive position of U.S. aircraft manufacturers.

Technology validation represents another area of concern. NASA's charter permits work in basic research on new principles, configurations, and structures. The charter also permits the next phase, which involves technology validation with near full-scale systems under representative flight or other simulated operating conditions. Technology validation is expensive, time-consuming, and risky and must establish irrefutable proof in order to meet certification and legal liability standards. As a matter of practice, technology validation work receives limited support from NASA, and adequate funds are not available to do more at present. Thus, a serious gap exists in the total process of developing and applying new technology.

The panel recommends reexamination of the research and technology development activity in support of civil aviation within NASA in the light of the changing competitive environment and the technological opportunities noted in this study.

The panel recommends reconsideration of NASA's activities and the resources available to support technology validation efforts with an eye to enlarging programs on validation and permitting work on advanced on basic design data on composites including consideration of manufacturing technology.

These programs should be closely coupled with strengthened mechanisms to ensure that areas selected for additional effort are relevant to the needs of industry and that the results can be applied with confidence.

Managing in the New Environment

The managers of aircraft companies face an array of threatening changes, e.g., weakened domestic customers, increased foreign competition, pressure to internationalize manufacture, escalating financial risk, need for capital, etc.

Four challenges warrant special mention:

1. Managing technological innovation to retain product leadership in the face of escalating costs for developing and validating new technology and growing uncertainty over market requirements and customer liability.

2. Developing new financial instruments and procedures that will help weakened customers purchase aircraft without undue exposure for the manufacturer. Ironically, innovative financing is becoming as important as innovative technology for this high-technology industry.

3. Learning to move from a position of global dominance to senior partnership with companies that have long chafed at the junior position in which U.S. dominance has placed them.

4. Developing the strategies for selective technological leadership that will permit overall systems leadership in a world where total leadership in technology is no longer practical. Achieving a lead position in an interdependent world will call for wisdom and vision of a high order.

Managing Human Resources

Aircraft manufacture is highly cyclical. The concomitant instability in employment is compounded by technological obsolescence that continually requires radically different skills. Thus, unstable employment affects professional, technical, and production workers. The assemblage of skills and working relationships in the aircraft manufacturing complex is a priceless national asset that must be preserved.

Workers and labor unions have long recognized the vital role of new technology in maintaining the health of the industry. Nevertheless, this industry, along with the rest of U.S. industry, has not yet developed adequate means of ameliorating the impact of wide swings in employment. It is vital to maintain mechanisms that will foster continued worker acceptance of new technology.

The efforts of foreign governments to stabilize employment are thought by some panel members to have been detrimental to productivity and effectiveness. Others believe that improvement in morale and receptivity to change create a net advantage. There is agreement, however, that three areas need urgent attention:

1. Retirement security--It is now possible for a worker to spend his entire career in the industry and never accumulate enough time with one employer to qualify for an adequate pension, an inequity that is counterproductive.

2. Unemployment--Management, workers, and the government have a responsibility to develop mechanisms for minimizing the impact of unemployment and for addressing the problem of the "migrant" skilled workers.

3. Training--Rapid technological changes place a premium on developing new skills and ensuring that workers share equitably in the fruits of technology.

NOTES

1. Throughout this book "recession" refers to the economic recession of 1980-1981.

2. Throughout this book the more generally used designation of Research and Development (R&D) will be used as an approximate synonym for the term Research and Technology (R&T) used within the aviation industry.

1
Overview of the U.S. Civil Aviation Manufacturing Industry

The civil aviation industry, including both manufacturers of aircraft and the commercial airlines, is in the midst of profound change. Some features of the change result from domestic actions and circumstances (for example, economic deregulation of air transport and the severe 1980-1981 recession), others from external developments (such as viable competition from Airbus Industrie in the large transport sector and erosion of U.S. industry leadership in international sales of civil helicopters, commuter aircraft, and business aircraft). The long-term implications of these changes are by no means clear. What is clear is that the stakes are of national importance because civil aviation is unique. Few other industries combine in as large a measure a crucial role in national security, a major contribution to national economic health and foreign trade, and a flagship role in the global posture of technical leadership accorded the United States.

This study focuses on aircraft manufacture, but its connection with civil air transport is so close that some current and prospective features of the latter must be included. Full assessment also requires examination of the relationship of civil industry to military activity.

The civil aviation manufacturing industry can be divided into two broad categories. One comprises large aircraft and their parts, jet engines, and avionics and support equipment used in national and international air transport. The other is more heterogeneous--including rotorcraft, regional transport, business aircraft, and light piston aircraft and their parts, avionics, and engines. This study covers both categories and notes where findings and recommendations do not apply to both.

18

TABLE 1-1   Civil Aircraft Shipments, 1968-1982
(millions of dollars)

Year	Total	Transport Aircraft	Helicopters	General Aviation
1968	4,267	3,789	57	421
1969	3,598	2,939	75	584
1970	3,546	3,158	49	339
1971	2,984	2,594	69	321
1972	3,308	2,660	90	558
1973	4,665	3,718	121	826
1974	5,091	3,993	189	909
1975	5,086	3,779	274	1,033
1976	4,592	3,078	285	1,229
1977	4,451	2,649	251	1,551
1978	6,458	4,308	328	1,822
1979	10,644	8,030	403	2,211
1980	13,058	9,895	656	2,507
1981	13,223	9,706	597	2,920
1982	8,610	6,246	365	1,999

SOURCE: Aerospace Industries Association of America, Inc.,
Aerospace Facts and Figures, 1983/1984, p. 34.

THE INDUSTRY AND ITS IMPORTANCE TO THE ECONOMY

The civil aviation manufacturing industry is a major component of the aerospace industry, which in turn is one of our largest
and most technology-intensive industries.   R&D expenditures,
including both company and government funds, for aerospace (the
only segment for which the National Science Foundation provides
R&D to sales data), represent 15.4 percent of sales compared with
3.3 percent for all manufacturing.

Shipments of large transports, helicopters, and general aviation aircraft are shown in Table 1-1. The variability of output for
a major capital expenditure such as aircraft is reflected in the
figures. Even within manufactured durable goods, commercial
sales of aircraft (including exports of military aircraft) vary from
just over 1 percent to more than 2 percent (Table 1-2). Although
transport aircraft represent the dominant factor in the industry,
sales of helicopters and general aviation have been growing more
rapidly, as also shown in Table 1-1.

The industry is an important source of employment for both
skilled production workers and for highly trained scientists and
engineers, who represent 16 percent of the work force (Table
1-3). Again, the highly cyclical nature of the industry is reflected
in the wide swings in employment. The employment data in Table
1-3 are conservative in that they include only estimates of aero-

TABLE 1-2 Comparison of Civil Aircraft with Gross National Product, 1970-1982, and Manufactured Durable Goods

| | Billions of Dollars | | | Civil Aircraft | Percent of |
Year	GNP	All Manufacturing	Durable Goods	(millions of dollars)	Durable Goods
1970	992.7	633.7	338.6	5,880	1.74
1971	1,077.6	671.1	359.7	5,079	1.40
1972	1,185.9	756.5	408.5	5,199	1.27
1973	1,326.4	875.4	476.4	6,739	1.41
1974	1,434.2	1,017.9	531.0	7,560	1.42
1975	1,549.2	1,039.4	524.1	7,797	1.48
1976	1,718.0	1,185.7	608.4	7,622	1.25
1977	1,918.0	1,330.1	696.1	7,530	1.08
1978	2,163.9	1,496.6	798.1	10,581	1.32
1979	2,417.8	1,727.3	909.6	16,023	1.76
1980	2,633.1	1,845.9	936.0	20,097	2.15
1981	2,937.7	1,994.6	1,001.0	21,527	2.15
1982	3,059.3	1,886.0	918.2	17,338	1.88

SOURCE: Survey of Current Business, U.S. Department of Commerce, Aerospace Industries Association of America, Inc., Aerospace Facts and Figures, 1983/1984, p. 30.

space-related employment in communications, instruments, and selected other industries at the 2-digit Standard Industrial Classification (SIC) level. Data on the massive 15,000-firm infrastructure that supports the industry are unobtainable.

Foreign sales are increasingly important to the industry, representing approximately 60 percent of large transport sales, 50 percent of rotorcraft, and 25 percent of general aviation. U.S. exports of large transports represent approximately two-thirds of total sales in the rest of the world. Civil aircraft play a major role in foreign trade, representing 4.2 percent to 7.1 percent of total merchandise exports since 1970 (Table 1-4)--highest of all export categories. Although the percentages vary, they seem to represent a relatively stable portion of the total. Even though imports of aircraft appear to have escalated dramatically in 1981-82, they are modest compared with exports (Tables 1-5a and 1-5b). Figure 1-1 shows the growth of imports since 1970 for large transports, helicopters, and general aviation aircraft. The increase in imports is troublesome, but year-to-year variations can be large and no conclusions can yet be drawn about trends with respect to large transports. The situation in helicopters and general aviation is quite different. As can be seen in Table 1-5a, penetration of imports is escalating rapidly.

Exports of transports are a major part of total aircraft exports. The great importance of the extensive fleet of U.S.-built aircraft operated by foreign airlines is reflected in the large sales of aircraft and engine parts (Table 1-5b).

TABLE 1-3 Employment in Aircraft Manufacturing,
1972-1982 (thousands)

Year	Total	Production Workers	Scientists and Engineers
1972	494.9	266.2	70.8
1973	524.9	284.2	72.1
1974	539.4	291.9	70.6
1975	514.0	271.1	67.5
1976	487.1	250.7	66.9
1977	481.7	246.8	72.0
1978	527.2	275.4	82.0
1979	610.8	332.1	86.5
1980	632.3	354.6	85.9
1981	648.9	344.6	95.2
1982	611.8	309.9	95.3

SOURCE: U.S. Bureau of Labor Statistics: Employment and
Earnings (Monthly), U.S. Department of Labor. National
Science Foundation.

This U.S. export trade contributes significantly to the strength
and cost-effectiveness of the U.S. aerospace manufacturing industry. A loss in foreign trade can have significant impact on U.S.
jobs and the economy. It has been estimated that every $1 billion
increase in aircraft exports could provide the equivalent of 16,490
direct and indirect full-time job-years per year in the 1982 to 1990
period. Of this number, 4,910 persons would be employed directly
in the aircraft industry. In addition to the $1 billion in sales,
follow-on orders of aircraft and spares would provide estimated
sales totaling $6.5 billion in the 1982 to 1990 period.[1]

ECONOMICS OF THE INDUSTRY

The manufacture of civilian aircraft, especially large commercial transports, is a long-term, high-risk, multibillion-dollar
venture. The lead times required are on the order of four years
for the aircraft and six years for the jet engine to power it. Since
the expected life of the aircraft in the manufacturer's product
line is approximately 15 years, the market at which the product is
aimed may be 5 to 20 years in the future, i.e., long after the key
product decisions are made. Only very gross data on economic
growth, air travel, and cost of capital and fuel are available.
Estimates contain huge amounts of uncertainty. Nevertheless,
the aircraft manufacturer must risk $2 to $5 billion with the high
probability that even a successful venture will not break even in
terms of cash flow for at least 10 to 15 years. The jet engine

TABLE 1-4   U.S. Exports of Civil Aircraft, 1970-1983 (millions of dollars)

Year	Total Merchandise Exports	Transport Aircraft	Other Civil Aircraft and Products	Total Civil Aircraft and Products	Percent of Total Merchandise Exports
1970	42,590	1,283	1,233	2,516	5.9
1971	43,492	1,567	1,513	3,080	7.1
1972	48,959	1,119	1,835	2,954	6.0
1973	70,246	1,664	2,124	3,788	5.4
1974	97,144	2,655	2,618	5,273	5.4
1975	106,561	2,397	2,927	5,824	5.0
1976	113,666	2,468	3,209	5,677	5.0
1977	119,006	1,936	3,113	5,049	4.2
1978	141,228	2,558	3,460	6,018	4.3
1979	178,798	4,998	4,774	9,772	5.5
1980	216,672	6,727	6,521	13,248	6.1
1981	228,961	7,180	6,132	13,312	5.8
1982	207,158	3,834	5,774	9,608	4.6
1983	195,969	4,683	5,912	10,595	5.4

SOURCE: U.S. Bureau of the Census, "U.S. Exports, Schedule B, Commodity by Country; Highlights of U.S. Export & Import Trade."

manufacturer must invest an additional $1.5 to $2 billion with his return being dependent on the success of the aircraft.

The financial record of commercial transport manufacturers since World War II is not reassuring. Only 5 of 22 manufacturers of large transports survive in the free world, and the viability of some of them is questionable. Furthermore, the profitability is below the average for all of manufacturing. The industry is subject to major swings in sales, employment, and earnings that create great difficulty in building and maintaining competitive development, design, and production teams.

TECHNOLOGY BASE

The technologies that underlie U.S. leadership in aircraft manufacture play a critical role in the total constellation of our technological leadership. These technologies include not only the more obvious ones that affect aircraft performance--aerodynamics, propulsion, advanced structures, and avionics and control--but also system integration in the design and manufacture of complex, high-performance equipment; project management to meet demanding targets for performance, cost, and delivery; sophisticated manufacturing techniques for fabrication, testing, and assembly; and computer-integrated manufacture, factory automation, and large-scale integrated information processing. Strength in these technologies diffuses throughout

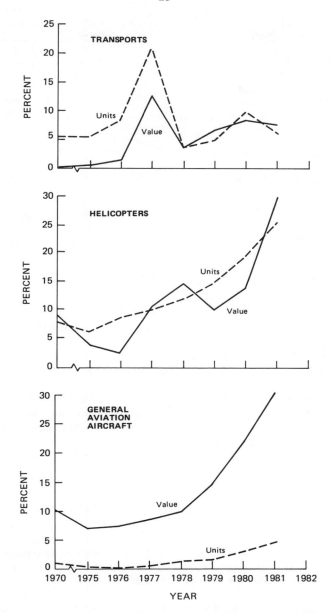

FIGURE 1-1 Imports of Civil Aircraft as Percentage of U.S. Consumption (U.S. production minus exports, plus imports).

SOURCE: U.S. Department of Commerce.

TABLE 1-5a   U.S. Civil Aircraft Imports, 1978-1983 (millions of dollars)

	1978	1979	1980	1981	1982	1983
Civil aircraft total	284.5	508.6	969.1	1,336.2	1,266.0	892.2
Transports	58.1	199.8	285.5	195.5	231.4	188.0
General aviation	146.8	260.4	495.8	913.0	837.7	541.9
Helicopters	28.0	21.6	53.9	105.4	84.9	89.5
Other	51.6	26.8	133.9	122.3	112.0	72.8
Civil aircraft Engines and parts	–	–	534.7	1,407.3	1,255.9	1,074.0

SOURCE: U.S. Bureau of the Census, Schedule B, Commodity by Country.

TABLE 1-5b   U.S. Civil Aircraft Exports, 1978-1983 (millions of dollars)

	1978	1979	1980	1981	1982	1983
Civil aircraft total	6,018	9,772	13,248	13,312	9,608	10,595
Transports	2,558	4,998	6,727	7,180	3,839	4,683
General aviation	496	650	739	790	517	356
Helicopters	156	207	299	346	206	232
Other	277	875	556	784	783	420
Civil aircraft Engines and parts	2,116	3,220	4,436	3,915	3,997	3,954

SOURCE: U.S. Bureau of the Census, Schedule B, Commodity by Country.

industry and contributes substantially to the overall strength and competitiveness of the U.S. economy. Furthermore, the experience gained from operating and maintaining a large, heterogeneous, intensively utilized commercial air fleet in itself constitutes a valuable technological resource that contributes to the national economy and security. These are some of the very reasons that foreign governments, both developed and developing, have targeted aviation as an important component of more general economic development programs.[2]

CONTRIBUTION OF THE INDUSTRY
TO NATIONAL SECURITY

A recent U.S. Office of Science and Technology Policy (OSTP) study highlighted the importance of aeronautics to national security.[3] Among the key findings of the study were the following:

• The United States depends heavily on technical superiority of military aircraft for national defense--approximately one-third of the Department of Defense (DOD) budget is for procurement, maintenance, and operation of aeronautical systems.

• A healthy, competitive civil aeronautics manufacturing industry reduces the cost of providing an essential military-industrial base and wartime mobilization surge capacity.

The contribution of civil aircraft manufacture to the military-industrial base is provided principally in two ways. First, the teams that could develop and apply new design and production technology to new military aircraft are kept in a high state of readiness by the continuing requirements of the civil market, which in normal times accounts for some 80 percent of the total production weight of aircraft produced. The design and production techniques and systems developed in civil operations can be, and are, transferred to the defense sector.

Second, the massive production base that is marshalled to manufacture civil aircraft is available as a wartime surge capacity. The many diverse items needed to manufacture a modern jetliner involve contributions from some 15,000 components manufacturers and materials suppliers. The items range from complex subassemblies and engines to avionics, electrical equipment, hydraulic and mechanical equipment and interiors, to nuts, bolts, and rivets. The skills and equipment needed are easily adapted to the production of military aircraft.

Military requirements for new aircraft would not in themselves provide a sufficiently stable load to maintain the design and production teams in an adequate state of readiness for emergencies. The deterioration or disbanding of these teams would represent a strategic loss that would not quickly be repaired, no matter how serious the emergency. In addition, the cost benefits that come from shared overhead would be lost. These teams include not only the most visible top layer of scientists and engineers associated with design, but also thousands of skilled design, development, and production specialists working on such things as the development and production of components, sophisticated materials, advanced propulsion systems, electronics, controls, communications, and machine tools, as well as tens of thousands of skilled production workers. This vast network remains viable only if it is constantly challenged and employed. Civil aircraft manufacture provides the base load of work for this network. Civil aviation manufacturing also provides available, off-the-shelf aircraft for mission support for U.S. defense.

Furthermore, the competitive drive for efficiency stimulates improvement in the productivity of this infrastructure by devising new machines and techniques for production, from which the military establishment also can benefit. This improvement occurs, of course, only if the aircraft industry is sufficiently profitable to be able to afford new equipment and training. This readiness-to-serve capability helps reduce the start-up costs and time that would otherwise be incurred in expanding capacity in an emergency.

If this development and production infrastructure deteriorates—as it inevitably will if the U.S. aircraft industry (or its civil customer base) is not financially healthy—the defense establishment will undoubtedly do whatever is necessary to help maintain the industry at an adequate level. Consequently, it is in the vital interest of the United States to ensure a healthy aircraft industry and to achieve effective coupling between defense and civil plans and programs where there is opportunity to benefit from such coupling. (Needless to say, our NATO partners also benefit from a healthy U.S. aircraft manufacturing industry.)

Rotorcraft represent a special case. Civil helicopters have been principally derivatives of aircraft developed for military use. But new third-generation U.S. military helicopter developments have not yielded aircraft suitable for civil certification and commercial use. DOD has in general recognized the values of commonality with commercial products in providing increased economies of scale and logistics, but its helicopter commonality policy has not considered the additional values that derive from inclusion of civil-certificated derivatives of military helicopters. New military requirements have created such specialized aircraft that they have limited commercial attractiveness to the market.

REASONS FOR PAST SUCCESS OF THE INDUSTRY

The U.S. aviation industry has dominated world markets since the end of World War II. It is important to understand the reasons for this success before examining some of the trends that are now generating concern. Part of the success results from the large-scale technology and production resource created for World War II. Additional powerful factors that have been decisive in establishing and maintaining U.S. dominance are: (a) a productive, decades-long relationship among the government, the major airlines, and the aircraft manufacturers in the context of a free market economy; (b) a combination of economic and geographical considerations in the United States that has favored air transport over other modes of transportation; (c) the size, diversity, and rapid growth of the U.S. air transport industry that provided a major domestic market; (d) an aggressive, effective program of technology development combined with an advanced, productive aircraft design and manufacture capability that received continuing infusions of resources; and (e) a system of product support that earned customer loyalty. These factors and relationships, including the productive linking of government to manufacturers and airlines, began as early as World War I. The National

Advisory Committee for Aeronautics (NACA) at its Langley Center, the Army at Wright Field, and the Navy Bureau of Aeronautics established the basic foundation for aeronautical and propulsion technology. The U.S. Post Office contributed significantly by establishing transcontinental airmail service via lighted airways in 1924, and the Kelly Bill in 1925 encouraged private investment in air mail contracts.

The modern structure of the industry began to emerge in 1934, with the separation of airlines from manufacturers by government fiat to increase competition and industry development. Direct subsidies to promote passenger travel, economic regulation of airlines, air traffic control, and safety authority were fully codified in the 1938 legislation establishing the Civil Aviation Administration (CAA) within the U.S. Department of Commerce. The functions of the CAA were divided in 1948. Two separate agencies, the Civil Aeronautics Board (CAB), and the Federal Aviation Administration (FAA) were established. The CAB was assigned to handle route and economic matters (economic regulation). The FAA was charged with technical, safety, and certification matters. Both were charged with encouraging the expansion of the industry. The combination of the NACA, Army Air Corps, and Navy technical research in aerodynamics, structures, engines, and fuels, together with R&D by private manufacturers and the development of far-flung airline operations, assisted the United States in becoming the world leader in commercially successful aircraft (e.g., DC-3) and services (e.g., extensive domestic routes and long-range overseas routes using the China Clipper).

U.S. civil aircraft, and especially engines, benefited from the continuous stream of large R&D investment by the military establishment, especially the competition for jet bombers. They also benefited from the economy of scale afforded by the growing domestic market, and from the aggressive, market-focused management of the industry. U.S. civil aircraft offered excellent performance, excellent quality and reliability, size and performance range that matched market needs, lower operating costs than European aircraft, competitive purchase prices, and excellent logistics and field operations support. European manufacturers sometimes led in introducing new technology, e.g., first use of jet engines in commercial transports and first smaller two-engine jets, but they did not succeed in marshalling the array of competitive factors that led to commercial leadership.

The principal reasons for the past success of U.S. large transport aircraft manufacturers have been a strong technological base, a good perception of airline and business requirements, and a willingness to accept the risk of implementing new technology and to tool up for early high production rates so that the market opportunity could be exploited as rapidly as it developed. United

States manufacturers have been able to make decisions about product selection, prices, costs, and production facilities with relatively limited government involvement, in contrast to their counterparts in Europe where governments have often been involved, e.g., the VC10 and the A300.

Business aviation directly benefited from the large U.S. technology base developed for commercial jet transports, described above. In the early 1960s business aviation was a small U.S. industry. Some large corporations had flight departments and recognized the benefits of rapid air transportation, but the fleet was composed of reconstructed military aircraft and a few cabin-class, twin-engined, piston-powered aircraft. Turboprops and jets were just being introduced.

In the ensuing 20 years progress has been enormous, due to rapid technological advances in U.S. aircraft design and manufacture, U.S. government support for small airports and navigation infrastructure, and the willingness of U.S. general aviation manufacturers to accept the risk in applying new technology in new products. As the market developed--helped by the expansion of industry and growth of small population centers--general aviation manufacturers frequently offered aircraft with much improved performance and service capability through advances such as high-bypass engines, increasingly useful avionics, long-range navigation systems, and structural and safety advances. Most other regions of the world had neither the domestic market, technological base, nor the government support that the United States enjoyed, and thus little competitive foreign industry developed in general aviation until the last half of the 1970s.

NOTES

1. National Benefits of Aerospace Exports, The Aerospace Research Center, Aerospace Industries Association of America, Inc., Washington, D.C., June 1983.

2. F.J.L. Diepen, "Aviation and Technology in the European Economy," AICMA-Symposium, London, September 13-14, 1967.

3. Aeronautical Research and Technology Policy, Executive Office of the President, Office of Science and Technology Policy, Volume 1: Summary Report, November 1982.

2
The Present Environment

The environment began to change in the mid-1970s. A series of events, both domestic and international, has altered the U.S. outlook. Evaluating the significance of these events and predicting the emerging trends is complicated by the deep recession of 1981-1982 that has affected civil air travel and aircraft procurement worldwide. The events of special note include: uncertainties in the financial status of U.S. airlines resulting from an inability to match revenues to increases in operating costs and deregulation of routes and fares; growing emergence of serious foreign competition in aircraft manufacturing; increasing importance of international markets; escalation of financial risks in the development, manufacture, and marketing of new aircraft; internationalization of aircraft manufacture; and foreign government involvement--some would say participation--in the industry.

CHANGES IN U.S. AIR TRANSPORTATION

System Development

The modern U.S. air transport industry evolved in the decade immediately after World War II. It comprised a small group of major carriers that were the launch customers for new aircraft, augmented by a group of other growing carriers that tended to be followers and a group of unscheduled charter operators with older equipment that emphasized low fares and minimum service. As in other countries, U.S. government regulation through the CAB controlled routes and fares. Consequently, airline competition concentrated on lobbying for attractive new routes and provision of more attractive passenger service, i.e., convenience of schedule and in-flight amenities. Fares were based on average costs, which continued to decrease as the size and efficiency of each new transport airplane improved the cost performance of the fleet. Because of CAB regulation the major airlines engaged in almost no fare competition to achieve lower costs through modifications in service or economies in airline operation. They did little to probe customer preferences by experimentation in fares or levels of service. The major airlines, not surprisingly, resisted both the entry of new airlines and attempts of smaller commuters to expand routes and service, even though they themselves were not aggressive in serving low-density locations that did not provide an attractive basis for profitable operations. Lack of competition in fares and service, combined with pressure of smaller operators to expand, is credited with creating an environment that fostered demands for deregulation.

Airline Restructuring--Deregulation

The rapid increase in fuel costs after the Organization of Petroleum Exporting Countries (OPEC) crisis in 1973 was a jarring note to the financial performance of the airlines. These escalating fuel costs changed the cost structure and operating characteristics of the industry. In the early 1970 the cost of fuel as a percent of total operating expenses was 12.7 percent. The cost began to escalate in 1974, reaching 30 percent in the early 1980s (Table 2-1).

A second major perturbation was created by deregulation. The termination of airline economic regulation in 1978 removed the

TABLE 2-1   Jet Fuel Costs, 1970-1982

Year	Cost Index (1972 = 100)	As Percent of Cash Operating Expenses
1970	93.7	12.7
1971	97.0	12.6
1972	100.0	12.0
1973	109.3	12.2
1974	208.0	17.4
1975	249.7	19.1
1976	271.6	19.5
1977	310.6	20.5
1978	336.8	20.1
1979	496.0	25.1
1980	766.1	30.5
1981	892.7	30.3
1982	841.6	28.1

SOURCE: Air Transport Association of America, Inc., Aerospace Facts and Figures, 1983/1984, p. 98.

barriers to entry and opened the door to new routes, new carriers, and unprecedented competition and flexibility in fares and services. Experience soon demonstrated that fare levels were more important to many people than service amenities. It is not yet clear, however, how many new passengers have been attracted as a result of lower fares because passenger statistics of this nature are limited and subject to various interpretations. The situation is further beclouded by the coincidence of a major recession.

During the era of regulation, short-range jet transport operation was traditionally subsidized by longer routes, with the level and degree of subsidization controlled by the CAB. Furthermore, the CAB provided direct subsidies for many short routes. These regulatory policies had the effect of creating an artificial marketplace in the domestic United States, which distorted operating efficiency and equipment selection to the disadvantage of some consumers--i.e., frequency of service was low to smaller localities; fares tended to be artificially high on the longer, more heavily traveled routes in order to subsidize the short, lower-density operations; and little was available in the way of specialized equipment to serve the commuter market because it did not appear attractive enough to stimulate the interest of aircraft manufacturers.

As the impact of deregulation began to be felt, the large carriers responded by abandoning their less productive, low-density markets. Commuter airlines, many of them new, expanded to fill the void. The number of certificated scheduled carriers offering passenger service has expanded from 36 to 98 (Figure 2-1). In addition, service in terms of number of flights and passenger seat-miles available has been increased for more thinly populated areas.[1] Perhaps more important, the structure of air travel service has changed markedly. The regional/commuter airlines have expanded the number of airports served, while the major national airlines have markedly reduced the number of airports served (Table 2-2). The trunk airlines have instead concentrated their attention on the largest hubs, where they offer competing service with majors already entrenched. Table 2-2 shows a 79 percent reduction in airports served exclusively by the majors and a 58 percent increase in airports served exclusively by regionals. Table 2-3 shows that in March 1983, 15 major carriers were serving only 42.8 percent of the city-pairs they had served in March 1978. The pairs dropped were replaced by joining other majors at a few major hubs. Figure 2-2 indicates the concentration of the major carriers on the large hubs. The sharp shift to the right of the lined bars indicates the dramatic concentration of major carriers at major hubs. At deregulation the average major hub was served by seven major carriers, by 1983 it was served by 10.

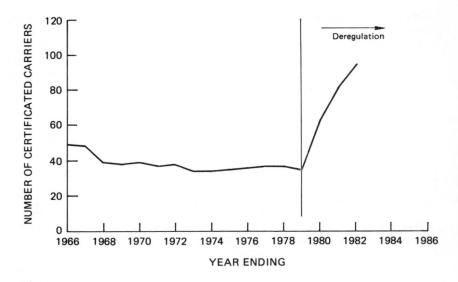

FIGURE 2-1 Number of Certificated Carriers Before and After Deregulation (Civil Aeronautics Board documentation of air carrier traffic statistics for September of each year)

SOURCE: Civil Aeronautics Board.

One study of airline productivity before and after deregulation found that average annual improvement for 10 trunk airlines increased from 2.6 percent between 1972-1975 to 4.9 percent for 1975-1980. Improvements for regional carriers increased from 4.0 percent in 1970-1975 to 6.3 percent in 1975-1980. The two categories combined showed an improvement from 2.8 percent to 5.1 percent. These numbers indicated a substantial improvement in productivity in the period including deregulation.[2] It should be noted that evaluation of productivity for a service such as air travel where convenience and time saved are important ingredients for many users, is exceedingly difficult. The study cited does not attempt to incorporate these variables.

The airlines have responded to deregulation by revising their strategies for designing routes. The earlier emphasis on nonstop city-pair routes is being supplanted by an expanded hub-and-spoke strategy. This strategy seeks to improve load factor by strengthening market positions in selected hub cities where airlines already have strong positions by funneling increased traffic in from other cities. Consequently, the number of major airlines serving major hubs has tended to increase significantly, while

TABLE 2-2 Airports Served by Regional and Major Airlines, 1978 Versus 1982

	1978	1981	1982	% Change 1978-1982
Airports served				
Regional/Commuters	630	766	817	+30
Major/Nationals	673	389	323	−52
Exclusive airports served				
Regional/Commuters	359	504	566	+58
Major/Nationals	230	80	49	−79

SOURCE: Fairchild Industries, Inc.

service to lower-traffic airports is increasingly being left to regional airlines; however, the number of nonstop flights between long-distance city-pairs is being reduced. Figure 2-2 shows the significant increase in service being offered by the 11 major airlines at the 25 largest hubs. Many of the major airports are now serving as key transfer points for passengers.[3]

Evaluation of the consequences of deregulation for the passenger depends very much on one's point of view, and both advocates and opponents have strongly held views. The panel has

TABLE 2-3 Major Airline Service Reductions Since Deregulation

Carrier	City-Pairs Served In		Percent of City-Pairs Served in March 1978 Which Were Also Served in March 1983
	March 1983	Both March 1978 and March 1983	
Northwest	284	165	58.1
Pan American	109	62	56.9
Eastern	503	273	54.3
Delta	645	335	51.9
Trans World	237	120	50.6
USAir	566	282	49.8
United	472	226	47.9
Piedmont	383	164	42.8
Ozark	208	83	39.9
Frontier	231	90	39.0
American	343	129	37.6
Western	253	86	34.0
Republic	945	305	32.3
Continental	384	59	15.4
Braniff	0	0	0.0
Total	5,563	2,379	42.8

SOURCE: Official Airline Guide, March 1, 1978 and March 1, 1983.

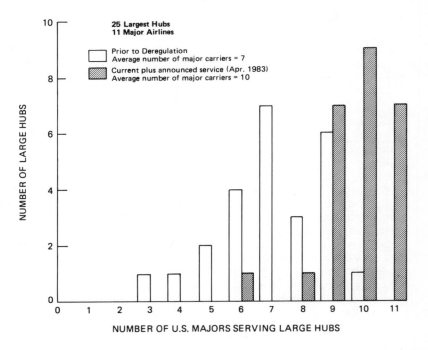

FIGURE 2-2 Concentration of Major Airlines at Large Hubs Before and After Deregulation

SOURCE: Official Airline Guide.

not attempted a comprehensive evaluation—it is beyond the scope of the study. The panel's perception of the various points of view is that for the frequent business traveler, chaotic fare structures and frequent changes have been unsettling; at the same time special incentive plans have offered him fare reduction. Furthermore, his interest in frequent point-to-point service between city-pairs is now sometimes less well served, (especially for longer-distance pairs) and in-flight amenities such as food and space have deteriorated. For the traveler who seeks the lowest possible cost and is willing to accept some inconvenience and minimal amenities, the result has been dramatic improvement. Travelers, both business and nonbusiness, in smaller communities face a mixed picture. For some, service is improved; for others, service is less convenient or nonexistent—commuter airlines, usually with propfan equipment, have expanded coverage; the trunk airlines have reduced it severely.

This change in route structure also changes the comparative demand for large versus small airplanes. For smaller route segments, the carriers need smaller aircraft. Consequently, there is a surplus of large aircraft (747, DC-10, L-1011) and increased demand for commuter airlines and fuel-efficient, 100- to 175-seat equipment. In fact, there is still considerable uncertainty regarding what mix of equipment will best serve future markets.

Depressed airline earnings and reduced demand for travel have created a pool of unused or underused aircraft, not necessarily with the lowest operating costs, but available at rock-bottom prices. Free entry and the absence of fare regulation make it possible for new operators to buy or lease such aircraft, select a high-density route, lease the operating infrastructure (ticket sales, baggage handling, maintenance), and hire otherwise unemployed flight and cabin crews at less than the salary scales of established major and national carriers. These new carriers obviously have very low costs in their selective route operations and can price their seats to be profitable at the margin for less than the established carriers, which have a large infrastructure, union salary scales and work rules, and the loan payments on highly efficient modern aircraft.

There are several consequences:

• Ticket prices stay low, driven by the lower costs of the new entrants, so that some established carriers continue to incur losses or nominal profits even as traffic grows.
• Operators find it more difficult to justify paying the high price of new and more efficient aircraft since the improvement in aircraft productivity may not outweigh the economic benefit of old, inefficient aircraft bought at discount prices and operated with low-cost labor.
• As new aircraft are bought by foreign, state-owned airlines, their used aircraft are taken in trade and frequently appear on the U.S. market.

The present period is one of transition, aggravated by the recent recession that further beclouds the future. The character of the eventual new equilibrium--assuming one ensues--is uncertain. More time will be required for the full effects of deregulation to become clear. Despite the pressure for improved efficiency in operations, the lower fares, and the improved service to some smaller communities that deregulation generated, one cannot yet conclude that the present arrangement is optimal. In assessing results, it is important for consideration to be given to all the significant effects, including safety and the impact on the aircraft manufacturers.

Irrespective of the details of the outcome, high priority must continue to be placed on safety. Even though the commitment to safe operations of all interested parties is continuously reaffirmed, it is important to reexamine all the institutional arrangements for insuring safety in the light of the changing character of the air transportation industry.

There is little question that the airworthiness of aircraft is subject to continuing careful scrutiny. During the era of controlled entry the professionalism, operating competence, and experience of the airlines with respect to such matters as flight crew training and monitoring, maintenance standards, replacement schedules, training and monitoring of maintenance crews, and depth and experience of engineering staffs were well established. The airlines then operating had been in business for many years and level of safety and reliability of schedules were major elements of the airlines competitive stature. However, with barriers to access removed it is important for the FAA inspection process to take into account such factors as the changed character of the industry, the many new entrants, the comparative lack of extensive operating experience and the variety of equipment utilized by given operations. For example, it is important to insure that severe cost pressures and the more heterogeneous fleets--with some flight and operating crews having to adjust to different instrumentation, flight deck layouts in aircraft, and work rules--do not lead to deteriorating standards of quality and safety. Accumulating experience has led to increased government attention to this situation.

Deregulation, depressed economic conditions, and growth of foreign competition are having profound effects on the U.S. manufacturers of aircraft. The subject is complex and multidimensional. One potentially disturbing effect concerns the continued capability of U.S. aircraft manufacturers to launch new aircraft. Depressed traffic and earnings of the airline industry have caused a severe reduction in new orders, deferment of deliveries, and in a number of cases, inability to take delivery of firm-order aircraft. The prospect of continued instability in route structure shortens the time frame over which forecasts can be relied upon for decisions on capital investment. It is difficult to make a decision based on a calculation of the return on investment of a new aircraft with a service life of 20 years when routes and traffic can not be forecast credibly for the next 12 months.

Although it is premature to make such a dire prediction, these adverse conditions could persist long enough to prevent the launch of new programs, cause the termination of current development and production programs, and lead to the disbanding of the teams performing advanced development. Such an eventuality would lead to a deterioration of aircraft design, development, and production capability in the United States with attendant adverse consequences for the military establishment as well.

Other nations, with economic and social criteria that do not apply to private U.S. firms, can and may seek to take advantage of recent changes in this U.S. market environment. Foreign programs to launch new aircraft could damage the prospects for future U.S. industry recovery. This subject will be discussed in more detail below under "Emergence of Foreign Competition." Monitoring this situation, and taking corrective action as need be, warrants the highest attention within industry and the government.

This "worst case" scenario could not be regarded as probable at the present time. However, very undesirable and costly deterioration could occur before the problem is perceived and adequately addressed if it is not watched carefully.

FINANCIAL STATUS OF THE AIRLINES

Major Airlines

For all major and for some of the smaller airlines, deregulation generated great uncertainty with respect to financial yield per seat-mile offered. It also produced an inappropriate match between the existing aircraft fleet and the evolving network of routes.

For many of the major airlines the consequences of these events, combined with a deep recession, have been a suboptimal fleet mix for hub-and-spoke routes, reductions in market share, serious deterioration in financial performance, dramatically different and heightened competition, and an urgent need to control or reduce frequently intractable operating costs.[*] Table 2-4 and Figures 2-3 to 2-5 reflect the decline from consistent profits to severe losses and the deterioration in debt/equity and working capital ratios, and breakeven points. Although these changes are obviously adversely affected by the recession, they began well before it and coincide with the onset of deregulation.

Perhaps the most important and uncertain elements relate to planning route structures and fares, forecasting financial performance, and projecting capital and equipment requirements for procurement of new flight equipment.

The changes noted above are very important to the future health of the suppliers of new transport aircraft. It has become more difficult to forecast market requirements, and the continuing ability of customers to accept and pay for new equipment is less certain. These changes have altered the investment climate and the prospects for adequate security and return on

TABLE 2-4 Operating Profit of
U.S. Air Carriers on Domestic
Operations, 1970-1983

Year	Millions of Dollars
1970	(1)*
1971	257
1972	493
1973	494
1974	785
1975	117
1976	575
1977	657
1978	1018—Deregulation
1979	129
1980	(6)
1981	(264)
1982	(736)
1983	NA

*Loss

SOURCE: Aerospace Industries Association of America, Inc., Aerospace Facts
and Figures, 1983/1984, pp. 88-89.

investment for the financial institutions that fund the purchase of
new aircraft. In a regulated environment the route franchise was
regarded as a valuable asset that provided security for loans.
Historically, new aircraft were funded by internally generated
cash and short-term and long-term credit from banks and institutional lenders. The sharp deterioration in financial performance
has dried up the former, and the reduced stability brought about
by deregulation, combined with poor profit prospects, has largely
dried up the latter. It is interesting to note that representatives
of the equity investment community are more optimistic over the
financial prospects of the airlines than are bankers who supply
credit and must be concerned with ability to repay loans on
schedule.[5] The financial results for 1983 have not been reassuring.

Recently the industry has been successful in raising funds in
the public market, but these funds have been used largely to cover
losses. Due to the uncertain profit outlook this source of funds is
no longer as readily available. The financial representatives on
the panel indicated that the debt leverage permitted in the future
will be scrutinized more carefully. New sources of funds and
possibly the development of new financial instruments may be
needed, but a return to consistent profitability is essential if
carriers are to be able to purchase new, more efficient aircraft.

As noted, the outlook for the domestic airlines to continue to

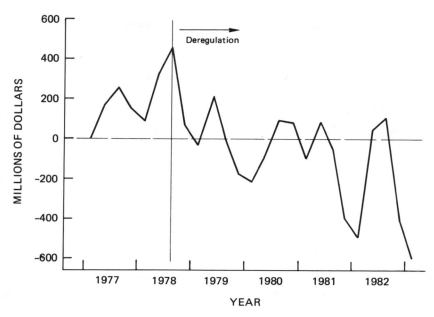

FIGURE 2-3 Domestic Operating Profit of the Major Airlines Before and After Deregulation

SOURCE: Civil Aeronautics Board.

serve as "launch customers" for new aircraft is clouded. An economic recovery with modest growth in air traffic has not yet resolved the problems of excess capacity, severe fare competition, and the need to reduce operating costs that continue to impair profitable operation. With respect to reducing operating costs, some airlines have taken drastic steps to avoid bankruptcy and have been able to achieve reductions in labor costs on a time scale that few familiar with the industry would have predicted at the beginning of the recession. A few are using bankruptcy reorganizations as a means to void labor contracts that have been a barrier to achieving cost-competitiveness. Other carriers will no doubt continue to experience liquidity problems that will inhibit their ability to finance new aircraft. The ready availability of low-cost used equipment will likely continue to make it easy for new entrants into even major hubs as long as noise regulations do not ground such equipment. It is also possible that carriers not experiencing significant financial problems will devote resources to protecting route structures by cutting fares to meet competi-

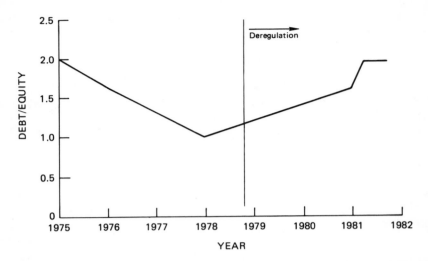

FIGURE 2-4 Composite Debt-to-Equity Ratio, U.S. Major Airlines

SOURCE: Presentation before U.S. Civil Aviation Manufacturing Industry Panel, July 7, 1983, by H.C. Munson, Boeing Company, Seattle, Washington.

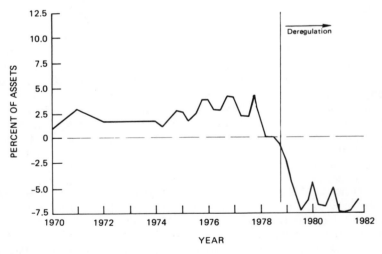

FIGURE 2-4a Working Capital Ratio, U.S. Major Airlines

SOURCE: Presentation before U.S. Civil Aviation Manufacturing Industry Panel, July 7, 1983, by H.C. Munson, Boeing Company, Seattle, Washington.

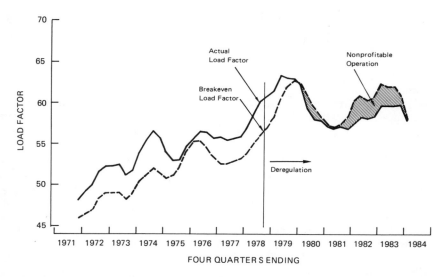

FIGURE 2-5 Load Factors and Breakeven Points of Major Airlines Before and After Deregulation

SOURCE: Derived from Civil Aeronautics Board data.

tion rather than risk commitments to new generation aircraft that may not meet competitive needs by the time of delivery.

The domestic airline industry may well continue to be unstable for some years. The failure of several additional major carriers is a possibility. It is likely that when the situation stabilizes the industry will continue to exhibit the characteristics now displayed, i.e., it will be made up of several financially strong carriers, such as American, Delta, and United, a number of marginal carriers, and a number of new entrants with varying financial strengths. The number of carriers comprising the latter group will probably vary with the economic cycles, with some failing and new ones entering. The financial health of the industry will be strongly affected by the success of airline managements and labor unions in achieving lower costs and higher productivity. The success of individual airlines will be strongly influenced by the marketing perception and nimbleness of their management in identifying and serving attractive market segments. They will operate in a much more volatile competitive environment. It is unlikely that many of the new airline entrants emphasizing low-cost operation, severe price competition, and great flexibility will readily take on the long-term capital commitments required to purchase new aircraft, much less to help launch a new aircraft.

Selected U.S. carriers with international routes may do somewhat better because capacity is, to some extent, subject to bilateral agreements with other countries. Although discounting is severe on selected routes, the international carriers are taking some steps to improve yields rather than expand market penetration.

If, as the panel postulates, a few strong carriers survive the competitive struggle created by deregulation, they could again serve as launch customers for new aircraft. In the near future the broad base of healthy airlines demanding new equipment, which the domestic industry has provided in the past, will probably not exist. Lacking such a platform to launch new aircraft models, U.S. manufacturers would have to depend more than they have in the past on financially stronger non-U.S. airline customers for initial orders. This change would undoubtedly alter the nature of competition from foreign manufacturers. If the foreign manufacturer is a multinational consortium with a good product the aggregate marketing power than can be brought to bear can be daunting.

It is not evident to the panel that the implications of deregulation of the airlines for the health and competitive status of the U.S. civil aircraft manufacturing industry have heretofore received adequate attention. It is important for future evaluations of the effect of deregulation to include this additional dimension.

Regional Airlines

The regional airline segment of the domestic airline industry is made up of approximately 245 carriers, serving regional areas with low traffic density and short route segments that are not economically attractive for the larger national and major carriers. In addition, these regional carriers often provide service to various connecting hubs in cooperation with the major airlines. The number of entries and exits from this segment is greater than that of the larger carriers.

Unfortunately, comprehensive financial data on regional airlines are not available. Most are not publicly-owned, and the few that are public have gone so only in the last three years. Members of the financial community have told the panel that typically the regional carriers are weak financially. Uneven earnings and cash flow, combined with weak balance sheets, do not provide a credible basis for supporting borrowings from conventional sources of financing for purchasing new aircraft (much less for supporting long-term commitments for developing new aircraft). Consequently, the burden of providing financing for purchase of new aircraft usually falls on the aircraft manufacturers. It has become apparent that the ability to offer a financing package, if one can afford it, is an essential marketing tool.

The change in route structure resulting from deregulation created an active demand for aircraft from the regional carriers, which currently represent a growing segment of the potential U.S. aircraft market. Some of the problems of low traffic and unsatisfactory yield that are prevalent among the larger carriers are also present with the regionals. Part of their poor performance, however, is due to the fact that the aircraft they are currently operating are not cost-effective for the routes served. Thus, if financing can be secured, there is a market for new existing or advanced aircraft. It is anticipated that as the economy improves, demand for the smaller transport aircraft will pick up before the demand for larger transports. The key is financing, which depends on long-term assurance of economic stability.

EMERGENCE OF FOREIGN COMPETITION

Large Transports

All nations are concerned with their balance of trade. The industrialized nations have evidenced a desire to participate in higher-technology, higher-visibility items such as jet transports. They recognize the advantages in exports, domestic employment, technology, sophisticated manufacturing, and prestige. Furthermore, they perceive the need to balance trade and national security by producing as much as possible of their military equipment needs domestically.

Not surprisingly, the Europeans have tried repeatedly to create a viable air transport manufacturing industry. The jet transport era was, in fact, launched with the British Comet and de Havilland Ghost turbojet engine in 1952. Over the next 15 years a succession of European firms and consortia built eight additional models of commercial jet aircraft, but with little commercial success. United States manufacturers addressed the interests of a diverse range of large, strong domestic customers and foreign airlines in their design deliberations. Thus, their aircraft matched the requirements of the United States and most international markets as well. Until recently, the combination of a large domestic market base, attractive products, and aggressive marketing and product support worldwide enabled U.S. manufacturers to dominate the large civil transport aircraft industry.

The European efforts were characterized by competing national, political, and economic interests, by lack of experience with customer-focused product planning, and by a narrower view of market requirements based on European experience. As they turned to multinational consortia to undertake development, the Europeans also encountered a lack of experience in managing such undertakings--a lack shared by U.S. manufacturers, and one they did not have to address until later. Despite the early European failures, those efforts provided many valuable lessons from which the present consortia have gained.

In December 1970, in response to the advent of the wide-bodied jets, the European transport aircraft industry was rationalized with the creation of a major European marketing project--Airbus Industrie--which draws on the aircraft manufacturers in a number of European countries.[6] The Airbus program, starting with the A300 airplane, has a strong market orientation that seeks to serve not only the European, but also the Asian, African, and South American markets, and specifically the large North American market.

In contrast to the competitive adjustments and structural realignment that have been occurring in the U.S. aircraft manufacturing industry over the past decade without specific government guidance, European governments for many years have had a strong hand in encouraging industrial realignments by nationalizing and combining firms within countries and by intergovernmental agreements for intra-European cooperation.

The Airbus A300 series of aircraft (twin-engined, wide-bodied jets) are technically proficient airplanes that have been more successful commercially than most earlier European developments. Their success has resulted in part from government financial support of design, development, manufacturing, marketing, and sales. In part, it also reflects the fact that the A300 addressed a market segment not well covered by U.S. aircraft. Until Boeing was able to deliver the 767 beginning in 1982, Airbus had the only advanced twin-engine, wide-bodied airplanes on the market. As can be seen in Table 2-5 Airbus has managed to achieve much more effective market penetration than the Europeans ever achieved in narrow-bodied jets. Although Airbus achieved virtually no market penetration until 1975, it has been a powerful factor in the market since that time. Airbus obtained 49 percent of the orders in 1980 and has obtained 36 percent of all orders since 1978, the year it began to demonstrate strong market acceptance. Unfortunately, data are not available on the financial performance of Airbus Industrie or on the level of investments or the criteria applied for evaluating performance and requiring payback to the various governments that are partners in Airbus. However, the investment is estimated to be about $5 billion. It is

TABLE 2-5 Market Share of Commercial Jet Transports by Type of Aircraft Orders

	Narrow-Bodied			Wide-Bodied			Total	
Date	United States	Foreign	Total	United States	Foreign	Total	United States	Foreign
1947-54	–	19	19	–	–	–	–	19
1955-59	409	154	563	–	–	–	409	154
1960-64	701	261	962	–	–	–	701	262
1965-69	2,079	283	2,362	346	–	346	2,425	383
1970	127	29	156	69	–	69	196	29
1971	105	34	139	41	6	47	146	40
1972	180	52	232	68	3	71	248	55
1973	210	21	231	65	–	65	275	21
1974	198	25	223	62	8	70	260	33
1975	121	30	151	31	15	46	152	45
1976	179	14	193	44	1	45	223	15
1977	221	12	233	76	20	96	297	32
1978	374	18	392	229	69	298	603	82
1979	221	12	233	194	127	321	415	139
1980	255	20	275	160	155	315	415	175
1981	191	29	220	124	80	204	315	109
1982	171	6	177	17	6	23	188	12
1983	139	–	139	41	2	43	180	2

SOURCE: Merrill Lynch Aviation Log.

known that Airbus survived for five years with only 10 orders after its announcement--something no U.S. company could do and remain in the business--and that it has built unsold aircraft ("white tails" worth $1.25 billion) to be placed in inventory during the recession, again something no U.S. company could finance. The competitive threat of such action is demonstrated in the recent sale of some of the "white tails" to Pan American. It is of course true that the overall program objectives and evaluation of success are quite different for Airbus, with job creation holding a high place.

The advent of deregulation, with the concomitant changes it has generated in route structures and service, has increased the importance in the U.S. of the market segment that Airbus serves. This market segment (moderate-range, high-density) has been served historically with many hundreds of early model BAC-llls, DC-9s, B-737s, and B-727s. Many of these aircraft, due to age alone, not to mention problems with fuel efficiency and noise, are candidates for replacement. Nevertheless, Airbus has had little success since deregulation in penetrating this U.S. market.

Airbus Industrie has been particularly successful in estab- lishing a foothold in the band of countries from the Middle East to South and Southeast Asia and to Australia, a region forecast to have the highest rate of growth in air transport over the next two decades. Airbus Industrie, according to its own public pronouncements, has the objective of obtaining a substantially enhanced market position in the 1980s. It has introduced the A310, in direct competition with the Boeing 767, to broaden its family of large transport aircraft.

In the coming decade the market changes noted above may lead the carriers to look for a new, more productive short-to-medium range aircraft with a seating capacity of 120 to 170 passengers. Such a vehicle would be a fuel-efficient replacement for older aircraft that serve short-to-medium range, moderate density routes. This market segment, however, has considerable uncertainties. The Boeing 737-300 and McDonnell Douglas MD-80 series (updated, enlarged versions of old designs) serve it in part, and now the Boeing 757 competes in the larger sizes. U.S. manufacturers are reluctant to launch an all-new airplane program until market requirements are clarified and potential customers identified with greater certainty. Nevertheless, the Airbus partners have agreed to proceed with the A320, aimed specifically at this market. Airbus hopes, by moving aggressively, to preempt U.S. manufacturers in this segment, and thus to capture a significant market share by being the first to offer a completely new aircraft of this size. The possible advent of the unducted fan jet engine in the late 1980s or early 1990s is adding further uncertainty and complexity to this competitive scramble.

After repeated attempts since World War II, Europe has produced an aircraft in the A300 that has achieved market acceptance in regions outside Europe. The effort has provided thousands of jobs, saved foreign exchange, and contributed to national prestige by demonstrating ability to produce a technologically proficient aircraft. The eventual success of Airbus in achieving worldwide market penetration with a family of aircraft is unclear, but its efforts to do so inject additional uncertainty into an already uncertain business outlook for U.S. manufacturers. Furthermore, through aggressive pricing and financing it can further reduce the investment attractiveness of the U.S. commercial aircraft industry, whose financial performance has been modest at best.

Rotorcraft

The U.S. industry's civil helicopter product line is matched in all significant classes and sizes by competitive foreign helicopters. Current competition is from individual helicopter manufacturers in France, Italy, West Germany, and the United Kingdom. Multinational competition is emerging. Messerschmitt-Boelkow-Blohm (MBB) of West Germany and Kawasaki of Japan have recently formed a joint venture. They have established cooperative development and production of the BK-117--a medium, twin-engined helicopter powered by Avco Lycoming LTS-101 engines.

In another multinational program, the governments of Italy and the United Kingdom have agreed to start a new 30-passenger, three-engine civil transport helicopter program. This aircraft, the EH-101, will be developed and produced by European Helicopter Industries, a consortium formed by Augusta of Italy and Westland of the United Kingdom. A military version will be developed concurrently for the British and Italian navies and for export. The EH-101 will be powered initially by General Electric T700 engines.

For a long time the U.S. civil helicopter product line consisted principally of derivatives of aircraft developed and produced for the U.S. military services. Most of the recently developed U.S. military helicopters are dedicated combat vehicles that do not provide a cost-effective opportunity for developing civil derivatives. As a result, the U.S. civil helicopter industry has had to develop and initiate production of its next generation of commercial products with private capital absorbing all business and technical risks.

U.S. civil helicopter manufacturers, operating on private capital, have to compete with financing granted (or guaranteed) by foreign governments to their helicopter industries. Using such capital as part of a basic government strategy to create jobs and business, helicopter industries in Europe have developed and introduced products that are aimed at the world civil market without having to incur the traditional business risk. (The U.S. domestic civil market represents about 50 percent of that world market.) These aircraft sometimes feature advanced technology acquired or confirmed through U.S. license agreements and reciprocal defense procurement agreements. They have had a large measure of success. The foreign share of the U.S. civil helicopter market, measured by shipments, has increased from 14 percent in 1979 to 35 percent in 1982 and is projected to continue to grow, unless the U.S. helicopter industry finds a better means of financing the development and initial production of competing products (Table 2-6). United States manufacturers of necessity

TABLE 2-6   U.S. Civil Helicopter Market (millions of dollars)

Shipments	1978	1979	1980	1981	1982
U.S.-produced domestic industries	172	196	357	251	159
Imports	28	22	54	105	85
Total Market	200	218	411	356	244
Imports share percent	14	10	13	29	35

SOURCE: Compiled from Aerospace Industries Association of America, Inc., data.

are moving to form joint ventures in Canada and elsewhere, on the basis that part of a loaf is better than none.

General Aviation

Unfortunately, the various categories of aircraft comprising general aviation are not always defined consistently and unambiguously. General aviation will be taken to include regional aircraft (often referred to as commuters), business aircraft for executive travel and other uses, and light (piston-powered) aircraft for both private and business use. Although the United States manufactures some 90 percent of the world's fleet of general aviation aircraft and represents the largest single market by far (two-thirds of total world demand), significant inroads are being made by foreign manufacturers.

In 1981 our trade balance in general aviation aircraft was negative due to imports of turboprop transport aircraft for the regional market and business jets (Figure 2-6), and the negative balance persisted into 1982 and 1983. It should be noted, however, that these imports have significant U.S. content in terms of materials, components, and subsystems.

Regional Transports

Regional transports (defined as commercial transport aircraft with less than 60-passenger capacity) present a bleak picture for the four U.S. manufacturers in this market, despite the fact that there is a strong growth pattern in this segment of air transportation. The financial, technological, and managerial requirements for launching these aircraft are less severe than for large transports. However, the investment needed is still beyond the capability of those U.S. companies normally involved, and the regional airlines are too small and too thinly financed to support launching-size purchases. This smaller investment for development is, however, within the capability of smaller economies and single nations. Consequently, in addition to Canada, the United Kingdom, France, Italy, Holland, Sweden, and Israel, the Brazilians, Spanish, and Indonesians also perceive this segment as a means of participating in air transport design and manufacture. Some of the programs in these countries are being undertaken as international partnerships. For example, the Canadian government has supplied Pratt and Whitney Aircraft-Canada with $130 million (Canadian) of R&D for the PT6--an engine for regional and business aircraft. Of this $130 million, $110.5 million was in the form of an interest-free loan; the rest was direct support.

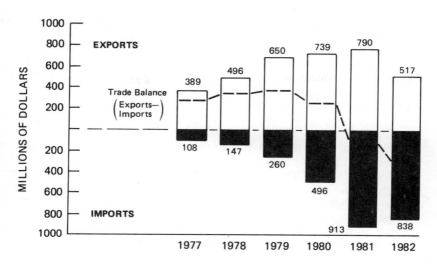

FIGURE 2-6 Balance of Trade in General Aviation Aircraft, 1977-1982 (general aviation aircraft, fixed wing of less than 33,000 pounds)

SOURCE: Aerospace Industries Association of America, *Aerospace Facts and Figures, 1983/84*, p. 132.

United States manufacturers estimate their engines could be priced 10 percent lower under comparable terms.[7] This level of activity is indicative of the importance and status attached to aircraft manufacture and to the growing commitment of many nations to participate in the industry.

The inroads appear to result from purchases of aircraft on which U.S. manufacturers have heretofore chosen not to risk development funds. U.S. regulation, both CAB capacity-limit rules and FAA certification rules, had for a long time suppressed growth of the regional market. Meanwhile, the rest of the world had developed a need for small (less-than-30-seat), turboprop transports. This need stimulated foreign manufacturers to pursue the development of this class of aircraft, e.g., CASA-212 (Spain, Indonesia) and Shorts-330 (United Kingdom). However, with low fuel prices and limited U.S. demand, total world sales remained low. Increased fuel prices and deregulation changed this situation. Regional airlines, which use efficient turboprop equipment for short-range operations, are now projected to grow significantly. Driven to a significant degree by the American market, the size of the aircraft needed has also grown. In the United States, only one company (Fairchild) has invested in an aircraft with a seating capacity of over 20 passengers. Fairchild produces a 19-passenger regional aircraft, the Metro, but for a 30-seat aircraft it has joined with Saab of Sweden to produce the SF 340, a twin-engined turboprop.

For foreign manufacturers, this market has the further attraction of not having a strong, established U.S. presence. In contrast to the situation for large jet transports, where the growing size of the international market means that the U.S. market is no longer the only basis for launch, the U.S. market is the single most important element of the decision to launch a turboprop aircraft. Sales in the U.S. are probably essential to the successful launch of a new regional aircraft because the United States comprises over half of the market potential. Furthermore, the U.S. market is open to all, whereas foreign markets are often politically controlled and access is generally limited. A U.S. aircraft manufacturer hence is in quadruple jeopardy: it begins with a limited presence in the market; its U.S. market is relatively open to competition; many foreign markets are totally closed; and a large number of foreign manufacturers (often supported by government financing) are concentrating on the field.

Business Aircraft

Business aircraft comprise a fleet of some 120,000 aircraft, of which 66,000 are used directly for business or executive travel. The remainder are used for a variety of lesser commercial purposes such as air taxi, rental, instruction, etc. In turbine-powered and turboprop equipment Canada, France, Israel, Japan, and the United Kingdom offer a significant challenge to the U.S. industry, and new groups from Indonesia, Italy, Spain, and Sweden are entering the field. At present about 60 percent of the market is in the United States. The U.S. fleet of business turbojet and turboprop aircraft has grown substantially. At the end of 1981 the fleet numbered 3,171 fixed-wing turbojets and 4,660 fixed-wing turboprops and was used principally for executive travel. Turbojets provide speed and moderate range. Turboprops offer, basically, operational efficiency. Foreign manufacturers have made significant inroads in the United States and world markets. However, about two-thirds of the current and planned turboprops are produced in the United States, two foreign-designed aircraft are to be assembled in the United States, and one (Learfan 2100) may be built in Northern Ireland from a U.S. design. Figure 2-7 displays shipments of regional and executive aircraft from 1970 to 1982.

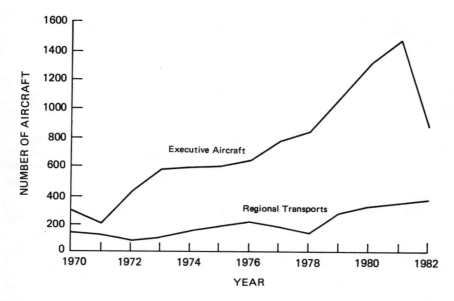

FIGURE 2-7 Shipments of Regional Transports and Executive Aircraft (turboprop and turbofan), 1970-1982

SOURCE: Garrett Turbine Engine Company.

Light Aircraft

In light (piston-engined) aircraft three American firms dominate--Cessna, Beech, and Piper. American firms produced 17,890 units in 1979. In 1980 they provided 92 percent of all general aviation aircraft and 67 percent of net billings, producing 11,877 units. Because of the worldwide recession they produced only 4,000 units in 1982, with continued slippage in 1983.

Although France is the second largest producer, with 591 aircraft in 1979, there is not yet a serious challenge in this market from foreign manufacturers. Britain, Brazil, and others are also producing light aircraft. Brazil, under license to Piper, has produced a broad range of Piper designs. The state of the art applied to the light aircraft segment of general aviation has been low, and costs are increasing in the United States due to reduced production rates. Consequently, the potential for foreign penetration of the markets serviced by U.S. manufacturers exists if foreign governments choose to finance an entry. Since the U.S. market is approximately 90 percent of the world market, no other nation could support a significant, aggressive light aircraft industry without access to the U.S. market.

Emerging Competition from Japan

The Japanese represent the latest potential foreign competitor. The Ministry of International Trade and Industry (MITI) has identified aerospace as one of the targeted industries of the future.[8] Furthermore, MITI has identified the building of capability to develop new aerospace technology independently as one of the two most important things for the industry's future. Japan has been acquiring modern technological and production capability through coproduction of military aircraft. It has ventured, with some success, into the business turbojet and turboprop aircraft markets with the Diamond-1 and Mitsubishi MU-2 aircraft. Japan itself is not a significant user of its own business aircraft. Almost all of its production is exported. Of the first 600 MU-2 aircraft produced, 450 were sold in the United States, 120 in other countries, and 30 in Japan. After an earlier commercially unsuccessful effort to introduce a commuter aircraft, Japan has become a subcontractor and venture partner with Boeing on the 767. In addition, Japan is participating in an international consortium with Rolls Royce, Pratt and Whitney, and German and Italian partners to develop and produce a new engine for the prospective "150-passenger" aircraft (described in Chapter 5). Part of the motivation for this venture appears to be to gain access to large-scale test and development facilities currently lacking. Another is the need to learn how to establish credibility in the marketplace. As noted earlier, Japan is also developing a civil helicopter with a West German firm.

The nature of Japan's long-term thrust is not fully clear-- prime, partner, or subcontractor. The MITI position is that the magnitude of the technological and financial risks dictates the use of international joint ventures. Gaining access to foreign markets will also require joint ventures, and furthermore, creating market acceptance for Japanese products may well require international partners with long experience and established positions. Were the Japanese to join forces with the Europeans, the competitive threat, both technologically and in terms of access to markets and capital, would be formidable. However, achieving a major role as an independent designer and manufacturer of large transport aircraft almost certainly will require a much more substantial investment by the Japanese government and/or industry in aeronautics R&D than currently is planned. For the next 10 to 15 years Japan probably represents a larger threat to major U.S. producers of large aircraft parts and components than to the principal aircraft prime contractors and assemblers. No matter what role Japan chooses to play, it must be regarded as a potent force in helping to shape the structure of the global industry in the decade of the 1990s and into the next century.

U.S. Content in Foreign Aircraft

The emergence of powerful foreign competition is not without its opportunities, especially in the sale of components and subsystems. Despite the desire of the Europeans to use their component and subsystem technology in the Airbus A300, many components throughout the plane (auxiliary power units and avionics are examples), as well as major parts of the U.S.-designed jet engine, come from the United States[9] However, this situation is changing. Airbus management is replacing U.S.-supplied components with European components where possible and practical, and the effort will be intensified on the A320.

At present the European component industry is small compared with that of the United States The panel believes it is competent but relatively high-priced. The industry could replace U.S.-manufactured equipment in foreign-built aircraft, should the policy decision be made to do so and capital invested.

U.S. components in other classes of aircraft also represent a significant part of the assembled vehicle. In addition to engines, the flight controls, radios and navigation systems, and aluminum for the skin are generally provided by U.S. manufacturers. The long-term concern is that the acquisition of significant airframe market share by foreign manufacturers will result in greater foreign interest and activity in the components market that could displace U.S.-manufactured products. Examples of this expanding interest are the involvement of Japan and France in large jet engines; of England, Italy, Japan, France, and Canada in small turbofan engines; and of France, West Germany, Italy, and Japan in avionics and controls. Furthermore, with the formal launch of the A320, the sponsoring governments (France, Great Britain, West Germany, and Spain) also agreed in principle to strengthen Europe in the A320's subcontracting and component supply.

The most critical step in maintaining U.S. leadership in components is to preserve its lead in total aircraft system concepts, design, development, and integration. This kind of leadership is heavily dependent on launching new aircraft at reasonable intervals. Without this leadership in systems, the future of the U.S. components industry, as it relates to civil aircraft, could face much more severe competition than has been the case heretofore. Military systems provide some relevant experience, but commercial requirements are sufficiently different that a direct focus on commercial development and design is regarded as essential.

Foreign Perception of Future Markets

A British perspective on world competition in commercial aircraft is that Boeing will continue to dominate the long-haul, wide-bodied aircraft market.[10] The medium- and short-haul market is viewed as "up for grabs." Airbus is being encouraged by its British partner to develop, over the long term, a family of equipment to enter this market. The commuter market is projected to be chaotic, with many players from both developed and developing countries and with a requirement to deal with fleet operators who are shaky financially and who will need significant operational support. Consequently, the commuter market segment is regarded with caution.

In summary, the two broad segments of civil aircraft manufacture face different circumstances regarding the changing nature of international competition. Large transports face a competitor, backed by the resources of several European governments, that has succeeded in achieving market acceptance. Despite penetration in some important markets, the long-term success of Airbus is not easily predicted. Its ability to affect aircraft pricing and profitability adversely is a more likely possibility. Even with the availability of government funds, the projected financial performance of the aircraft will, in the long run, influence government decision makers. The experience of the Concorde and the A300 has loomed in the background in discussions on funding the A320. Governments do not have unlimited funds. With conflicting demands for resources, continuing drains on treasuries will eventually receive careful scrutiny. Unfortunately, that eventuality is small solace to the private firms trying to compete. Meanwhile, the Japanese loom as a potentially powerful but largely unknown factor in the competitive arena.

In the other arena, especially with helicopters, commuters, and executive aircraft, the threat is more immediate. The aircraft fit better with the resources of individual countries and companies. The U.S. market is large, open, and attractive. U.S. technology and U.S. components are readily available. Significant market penetration has already been achieved.

GROWING IMPORTANCE OF INTERNATIONAL MARKETS

As mentioned previously, the size and dynamism of the U.S. air transport market during the 1950s and 1960s played a power-

ful role in establishing leadership for U.S. aircraft. The requirements and size of the U.S market helped define the aircraft
needed and, with effective attention to foreign needs and markets, provided economies of scale that helped establish world cost
leadership. In 1971 U.S. air travel represented 57.5 percent of the
world's passenger-miles flown outside of the USSR, its allied
countries, and the People's Republic of China. During the period
1950 to 1970, U.S. airline operators bought 67 percent of the
aircraft produced by U.S. manufacturers.

This situation began to change in the 1970s. Growth of the
more mature U.S. air travel market was the slowest of the seven
major world regions (about 5 percent a year versus an average of
about 9 percent elsewhere), and U.S. traffic dropped to a 40 percent share of the passenger-miles flown. Since the early 1970s,
the world market for large transports has reflected the slower
rate of growth of air travel in the U.S. The 40 to 60 percent split
in new equipment orders favoring the higher growth rates in
foreign markets is a reversal of market splits in earlier years.
Current market projections through the mid-1990s indicate a
continued gradual diminution of the U.S. share of world passenger
traffic (Figure 2-8). The traffic projections show the U.S. share
dropping from 40 percent in 1981 to some 36 percent by the
mid-1990s. Nevertheless, in absolute terms the U.S. market is
still the largest market, and it is projected to show significant
future growth.

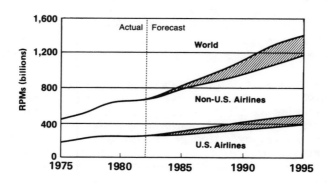

Note: Excludes U.S.S.R. and non-ICAO nations, but includes Taiwan

FIGURE 2-8 World Revenue Passenger Miles, All Services

SOURCE: Presentation before U.S. Civil Aviation Manufacturing
Industry Panel, July 7, 1983, by H.C. Munson, Boeing Company,
Seattle, Washington.

TABLE 2-7   Projected Growth in Air Travel

	Share of Traffic (percent)		
	1970	1982	1995
U.S.	55	40	36
Europe and Canada	29	31	31
Rest of World	16	29	33
	100	100	100
Revenue-Passenger Miles (billions)	288	678	1,413

SOURCE: Presentation before U.S. Civil Aviation Manufacturing Industry Panel, July 7, 1983, by H. C. Munson, Boeing Company, Seattle, Washington.

The less developed countries are estimated to have the most rapid passenger growth. The Middle Eastern, Latin American, Pacific Region, and Asian market segments are projected to increase from 29 percent in 1982 to 33 percent of total passenger service in 1995 (Table 2-7).

The success of a U.S. civil aircraft or engine program has always been heavily dependent on winning a large share of the international as well as the U.S. domestic market. The U.S. manufacturers have excelled in interpreting and satisfying the product requirements of international markets. But with the increased future importance of foreign airlines, the process of launching new aircraft or engines by U.S. industry will require even greater understanding of and responsiveness to the economic needs and political environment of foreign airlines and governments. These needs are well understood by our foreign competitors and have been exploited with great success by Airbus Industrie and Rolls Royce in opening markets for their current products.

Most foreign manufacturing competitors are backed by governments whose goals are full employment, technology development, and generation of foreign currency in addition to commercial gains. Consequently, these competitors are likely to stay in a selected market, even if large expenditures are required to sustain extended product development and production operations during periods of very slow sales--witness the experience with the A300 discussed earlier. While such actions would be both unsound and impossible for a private manufacturing company, they can make long-term social and economic sense for individual countries. Hence, this difference constitutes a formidable competition for privately financed U.S. companies.

Although the airlines around the world are experiencing problems similar to those of the U.S. airlines with respect to traffic, overcapacity, and yield, their general business situation is not as serious as that of the U.S. domestic airlines. The economic recovery outside of the United States generally lags behind the recovery in the United States, but traffic growth in many parts of the world has been more vibrant than in the United States even during the recessionary period largely because air transport is a less mature industry in the rest of the world. Fare competition for foreign operators, although more prevalent than in the past, is not as severe as for U.S. domestic operators. This is mainly due to foreign government regulation of fares, pooling of revenues, and control of capacity on routes between certain countries. On most domestic routes in other countries there is usually only one carrier, and any competition that exists is generally tightly controlled.

Most non-U.S. carriers are either government-owned or government-supported in some way. In developed countries there is a modest trend toward having the carriers stand on their own without subsidy or government-guaranteed financing, but not in developing countries. With few exceptions, such as Swissair, foreign carriers are largely instruments of their governments. Consequently, support is generally provided when it is truly necessary. Thus, when traffic makes the acquisition of new aircraft necessary, access to capital through government support is usually available irrespective of the financial performance of the airline.

For much of the international market, export financing is very important. Private sector banks are able and willing to lend or lease at reasonable terms funds for procuring aircraft by foreign airlines whose governments guarantee support for such transactions. In the case of developing countries, the financial condition of the airlines is usually weak, and the situation with regard to capital availability for purchasing aircraft is bleak. This group of carriers, while protected by bilateral agreements, often does not have adequate traffic to operate profitably on international routes. In addition, many of these carriers do not have a profitable domestic system.

Even though they are government-owned, carriers of developing countries have difficulty borrowing from the private sector to purchase aircraft even if the government guarantees the debt, because the country itself is in a weak credit position. Since the availability of capital for this group is uncertain, pressures are on the aircraft manufacturers to support these aircraft sales with help in financing. The availability of export financing is critical to this group of customers, but clearly there are increased risks in such transactions.

At a time when U.S. aircraft manufacturers face increased competition from foreign manufacturers, they also face a changing market. With the U.S. air transport system maturing, international markets will represent an increasing portion of the total.

Although U.S. manufacturers have always considered the interest of these customers, they must give them higher priority in the future, especially in launching new designs.

The subject of subsidies, and especially concessionary financing arrangements that are intended to influence purchasing decisions will be discussed in detail in Chapter 3. An explanatory comment is needed regarding the effect of exchange rates on the competitive position of U.S. manufacturers. The impact of a strong dollar on exports of aircraft is much less significant than one might postulate. Although in general a weaker dollar would no doubt be advantageous, two factors limit its effect. Most important is the commitment of foreign governments, and especially Airbus Industrie, to establish a position in world markets. The panel members actively involved in export sales believe strongly that Airbus will price competitively, irrespective of exchange rates. In other words, if the dollar weakened, Airbus prices (which are denominated in dollars) would simply be adjusted to compensate for the improved position of U.S. exporters. The significant U.S. content in virtually all foreign-built aircraft also dilutes the effect of a weakened dollar--foreign manufacturers must pay more in local currency for U.S. imports.

ESCALATING RISK

The development and introduction of a new aircraft has always loomed as a major undertaking. In the United States, the time from basic program commitment to certification and delivery for a large transport is four to six years, and a direct continuous outflow of cash totaling $4 to $6 billion is required before significant inflow of funds occurs (Figure 2-9). Recovery of the investment often requires 10 to 15 years. It may take decades if sales are slow or if the market demands derivative models. The engine manufacturer risks an additional $1.5 to $2 billion in developing a new engine over a six-year period. It is a risky business.

Justification of a new program has always required significant new technology, associated performance gains, and a defined market that can confirm the design goals and the necessary minimum volume of production. Competitive pressure may force commitment to variants of the design before delivery of the first basic model, making normal investment and risk still greater. "Betting the company" has been a frequent situation even for the largest companies.

Today, a combination of circumstances tends to increase risk still further. It includes a less predictable jet transport market, partially due to airline deregulation; an airline economic climate that demands maximum technical advancement, but also makes

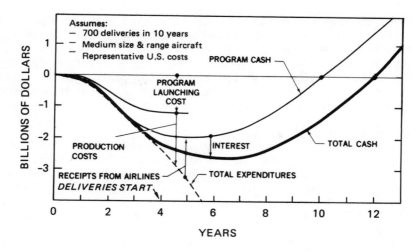

FIGURE 2-9 Typical Cash Flow Curve for Large Transport Aircraft Program

SOURCE: International Competition in the Production and Marketing of Commercial Aircraft, Boeing Company, March 1982. Based on curve from "Long Range Needs of Aviation," a report of the Aviation Advisory Commission, January 1983.

the financial ability to pay for what has been ordered less certain; and the escalation in product liability awards that is affecting all of industry. In addition, concurrent investments required for equipment and training, and for productivity improvement, may approach the development cost itself. And as noted earlier, strong foreign competition is emerging.

The use of new technology is an essential element of the total risk taken in the development of a new commercial aircraft. An advance in the state of the art is essential to be competitive, but if added performance is not achieved, or the advance is not cost-effective for the customer, or the product is delayed because of the new technical concept, additional costs are incurred and a share of the market may be lost. The risk is compounded by the need to make an early assumption about market share in establishing initial pricing. Any loss of aircraft performance or late aircraft delivery could reduce market share, precluding financial success.

An example of such a risk was the desire to achieve the weight saving and efficiency afforded by composite materials on the fan of the Rolls Royce RB-211 for the Lockheed L-1011. In the early

1970s the failure of this new fan and the necessary use of a backup titanium fan, with weight and balance changes to the aircraft, affected costs and schedules adversely. The change so perturbed the engine program that the Rolls Royce Company was subjected to financial reorganization. The impact on Lockheed included a forced hiatus in sales activity and near bankruptcy. Afterwards, the L-1011 program did not achieve sufficient sales and had to be terminated early because profitable future production levels could not be predicted.

Technical risk was obviously not the sole reason for Lockheed's L-1011 financial straits and program termination. The L-1011 was in head-to-head competition with an almost identical transport, the McDonnell Douglas DC-10. The ensuing competition forced unrealistic pricing levels on both airplanes. In addition, the worldwide recession so reduced the projected total market, and therefore both production rates, that pricing became even more unrealistic. Nevertheless, the failure to achieve a planned technical advance was a contributing factor in what eventually became a major financial loss for Lockheed.

The experience of the Canadair Challenger business jet illustrates the cost of delays associated with increases in weight and problems of engine performance that arose during development. Cancellation of orders and lost sales have resulted, requiring large additional capital investments that may never be recovered from sales.[11]

Conversely, failure to incorporate new technology can result in a vehicle that is not competitive and as a consequence cannot be successful. This situation is further exacerbated by the long time periods involved in design, development, and production.

Deregulation in the United States and the trend toward greater competition in foreign markets is causing restructuring of many airlines and worldwide experimentation with service, schedules, and routes and fare mix. The result is greater uncertainty regarding new product requirements, as well as decreasing prospects for large-volume sales of any one aircraft type.

In order to satisfy certification agencies and reduce their own potential for liability, airlines and aircraft manufacturers are incurring major additional front-end costs to "prove" a technology before it is introduced. In many respects the aviation industry is encountering, in magnified form, growing public requirements for utmost safety in all products.

Members of the Airbus Industrie consortium have stated[12] that they place great emphasis on the risk associated with airplane development and manufacture. This consideration played an important role in forming the consortium and in its decision to incorporate only proven technology in the A300.

The situation regarding risk is somewhat ironic because the understanding of technical phenomena, analytical procedures, testing, and operating experience that underlies present technology is clearly superior to that available earlier. It is the financial consequences of an error, or even a perceived error, that have changed.

INTERNATIONALIZATION OF AIRCRAFT MANUFACTURING

Given the situation described above, it is not surprising that since the end of World War II the number of prime free-world manufacturers of large commercial transports has decreased from 22 to 5. Competitors failing to capture sufficient market share have gone out of business or merged into larger entities. The massive infrastructure of vendors and subsystem suppliers who helped to spread the capital requirements of the U.S. prime contractors certainly contributed to their survival. One obvious response has been to spread the risk and the requirement for large financial resources by forming partnerships. In Europe this led first to national realignment of firms and then to multinational programs, principally among the nationalized industries of Great Britain, France, and West Germany, with each industry receiving the financial backing of its respective government. It also led to demands for offset manufacture of military aircraft among NATO countries to help build an indigenous production base and to generate the funds to buy aircraft.

This trend of increasing internationalization can also be observed among U.S. airframe and engine producers in the past 10 years. The joint venture of General Electric and SNECMA in engines, the Fairchild-Saab joint venture in developing the 340 commuter aircraft, the Rolls Royce engines on the Lockheed L-1011, and the involvement of Japanese and Italian firms as risk-sharing partners on the Boeing 767 are examples of growing foreign participation in the product development efforts of American firms. This same mode of operation is apparent worldwide--witness the General Electric and Pratt and Whitney engines on the A300, the 42 percent U.S. content in the British BAe146, and the 40 percent U.S. and 20 percent Canadian content in the Brazilian Bandeirante.

In addition to these joint ventures in aircraft and engine development, the export of U.S. components for incorporation into aircraft designed and built abroad has increased significantly. From 1978 to 1982 civil aircraft engine exports alone increased from $300 to $800 million and parts from $2.1 to $4.0 billion. The full extent of these exports has not been carefully examined.

Access to foreign markets and capital has also been a powerful motivating force for internationalizing the industry. Since many foreign airlines are state-owned, selection of aircraft for purchase is often subject to political review. Other considerations, such as the drawdown in foreign exchange, a desire to stimulate local employment, and the infusion of advanced technology, are weighed in these deliberations. Governments may demand off-setting arrangements as a part of the transaction. Consequently, a strong foreign marketing advantage can be achieved by forming partnerships, which respond to these additional criteria. The converse is also considered to be true. Failure to form such arrangements can reduce or eliminate market penetration.

The economic necessity for manufacturers to serve the total world market is conceptually illustrated in Figure 2-10, which shows representative effects on unit costs (of changes in produc-

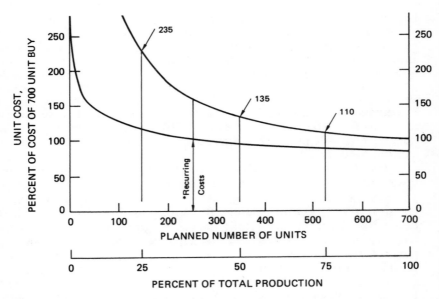

FIGURE 2-10 Importance of Market Size to Aircraft Production Costs

*Those costs directly associated with production of the aircraft, including manufacturing overhead. Remaining costs are associated with development, prototype testing, design, tooling, etc., prior to production.

SOURCE: McDonnell Douglas.

tion volume) for a projected fleet of 700 aircraft. A 25 percent reduction would result in a cost increase of 10 percent. A 50 percent reduction would result in a cost increase of 35 percent. If a foreign government elected to incur a cost penalty in order to establish a domestic industry that serves 25 percent of the world market, the effect would be to dramatically change the pricing and thus the profit prospects for a privately funded U.S. manufacturer. The 30- to 50-seat commuter aircraft market is a good example of such a possibility. With the opportunity for profit reduced or destroyed, due to a split market, the U.S. firm might well choose not to enter, and the foreign competitor would then have the total market available.

Other countries have made and will continue to make important contributions to aircraft and engine technology that U.S. manufacturers will want to tap (e.g., aluminum-lithium alloys, composite materials, electronic displays). International partnerships are an effective way of gaining access to such technology. The concept can work in both directions.

The relative merits of international partnerships are not easily judged. One must balance denial of access to a market and possible creation of a future independent competitor against at least partial access to a market, with accompanying risk that one may also be accelerating the development of technical competence by a partner--who may still eventually become a competitor.

Another complicating factor in evaluating the economic effect of the internationalization of the industry is U.S. content in "foreign" aircraft--a situation noted earlier. Today American manufacturers dominate the production of components used in commercial transports. It is believed this position will hold for the near future, but the longer term is less certain. U.S. firms manufacture the major share of engines, avionics, control systems, environmental systems, and auxiliary power systems used in aircraft in the free world, and much of the fasteners and aluminum from which the airframes are constructed. When sales to third parties of foreign airplanes with high U.S. content are taken into account, there can be a net positive U.S. foreign trade balance despite the importation of these same aircraft by U.S. customers. U.S. buyers, as well as third-party buyers of foreign-made aircraft, are purchasing parts manufactured in the United States--e.g., the A300 includes some 30 percent U.S. content in terms of value. In most cases (France is the principal exception) U.S. components tend to continue to be used on aircraft of foreign manufacture because local suppliers cannot afford the investment for the sales volume available domestically.

Internationalization of aircraft manufacturing has a number of additional important implications. One of the most significant is the evolution of a new skill in managing transnational technology development among partner firms. Until recently, multinational development programs in any industry, even within a single company that operated in more than one country, were considered very poor risks. The early difficulties in European cooperation in aeronautics reinforced the apparent validity of the perception. The success of the A300, the much smoother development of the A310, the productive partnership of General Electric of the United States and SNECMA of France, and the use of venture partners on the Boeing 767 all signify the change. The Europeans, and the Japanese for that matter, have accumulated much experience and management skill in such undertakings. The competitive value of such partnerships should not be underestimated. U.S. manufacturers, approaching such a relationship from a position of dominance, will need to demonstrate great sensitivity to the position and attitude of their potential partners. A number of members of Airbus Industrie perceive European companies as potentially more attractive partners for the Japanese than U.S. firms. Although this attitude may reflect some wishful thinking, it also reflects past experiences with U.S. firms that adopted a superior attitude in dealing with "junior" partners.

The use of consortia also has important implications for the nature of the industry itself. The major European partners in Airbus all began as relative equals in aircraft manufacture. They are evolving into specialists in portions of aircraft--wings, fuselage, control systems, flight deck, etc. Concurrently, project management, which was originally intended to rotate among partners, is solidifying in the Aerospatiale complex at Toulouse, where the major product integration and assembly work is located. Airbus is headquartered in Paris. With this increasing specialization--which is also fostered by the need to reduce technological risk--the role of the systems integrator and project manager assumes greater leverage. While a number of non-French representatives of the Airbus consortium have expressed concern about the long-term implications of this trend, they see no alternative at this point; nor do they perceive the eventual situation that may emerge. They have begun a journey because they felt they had no choice, but the destination is unclear.

The increasing participation of foreign firms as partners and major subcontractors in the development of new aircraft and engines by U.S. firms has led to similar expressions of concern over the impact of such arrangements on American technological leadership and on employment in the U.S. aircraft industry. Of concern is the increased opportunity such arrangements may provide for foreign participants to gain access to advanced American aircraft and engine technology. According to this argument, the more ready access of foreign firms to U.S. technology, in combination with their own technology development--to which (presumably) U.S. firms do not have access--can eventually imperil the technological lead of the United States. The recipients of the technology see the situation differently. Technology exchange agreements typically call for all improvements in the technology to be made available to all partners. This has been characterized as attempting to win a race with a rigid pole between the runner-up and the leader--the former's efforts only push the leader faster.

These concerns may reflect a misunderstanding of the basis for the current American technological lead and misconstrue the process and chain of relationships among research, technology development, and product development. The key to maintaining technological leadership is to sustain a vigorous R&D program, which generates a continuing stream of new knowledge and understanding. A particular product development extracts from that stream selected advances in technology to incorporate into the product. By the time that development is complete, the R&D effort, if it has continued, will have produced a rich additional stream of new knowledge. Making a particular embodiment available to a partner does not expose the underlying body of test data, analytical procedures, design principles, and related experience associated with its production. Consequently, while the product could be copied, it would provide limited information for creating a different embodiment and of itself would not give away leadership. The valid hazard against which one must guard is not that the technology might be given away by being embodied in a product, but that support for the long-range research and technology development might diminish, or of equal importance, that the United States might fail to develop new aircraft that incorporate the new technology.

The present status of U.S. technology is perceived by the panel as a mixture of both parity and leadership. Increasingly, the United States stands to benefit from, as well as to contribute to, partners who are technically advanced. The European partners in Airbus attest to the benefits derived from such partnerships. One benefit, perhaps not so obvious, is that the vigorous, often frustrating discussions that occur among partners help to minimize design errors before they get as far as hardware--even though the discussions may also lengthen the project. Undoubtedly, national pride also contributes to a sense of competition and a desire to "look good" in comparison with international partners. The negative side of partnerships is the building of potential competitors and the slower decision-making process that is entailed.

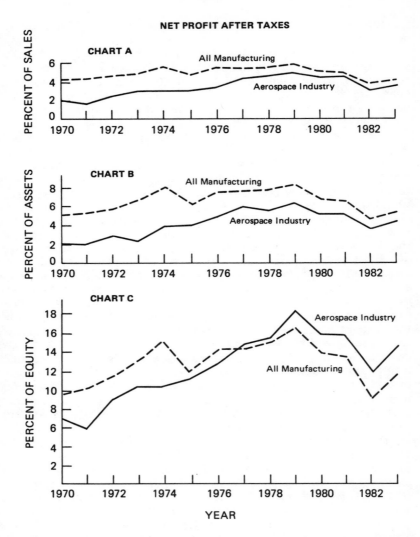

FIGURE 2-11 Financial Performance of Aerospace Industry, 1970-1983

SOURCE: Aerospace Industries of America, Inc.

FINANCIAL PERFORMANCE OF THE INDUSTRY

Analysis of financial performance of civil aircraft manufacture is very difficult because most of the important participants are also involved in military aircraft and other aerospace businesses as well. Data on civil aircraft manufacture are not developed on a continuing basis and current data are not available. The U.S. Department of Defense (DOD) made a hurried analysis for the period 1970 to 1975, but it is out of date and careful corroboration has never been carried out. DOD was expanding its procurement of military aircraft during that same period, and this too would affect profitability.

Data on the entire aerospace industry suggest a level of performance inconsistent with its image of leadership in high technology and its critical contribution to economic strength and national security. Charts A, B, and C in Figure 2-11 indicate a return on sales and on assets (a widely used measure of financial performance) that is significantly below that for all manufacturing. The crossover on return on equity in 1977 reflects in part the increase in debt financing that occurred during that period. The aerospace companies are more highly leveraged than formerly. As can be seen, aerospace financial performance has narrowed the gap with all manufacturing since about 1979. Inability to disaggregate data limits analysis, but it is known that many key industries, such as automobiles, steel, and machine tools, had disastrous performance that adversely affected overall profitability in manufacturing at the same time that military procurement was vacillating. Consequently, although the data are not conclusive, the panel concludes that profitability in civil aircraft manufacture has not been consistent with the picture of an industry that is technologically dynamic and has world dominance.

The anecdotal evidence on profitability is still more discouraging, even when allowing for the caveats about difficulties in disentangling the costs of a very long term project. The life cycle of a jet aircraft program is approximately 40 years (7 to 10 years of precursor R&D and design for the aircraft and the engine, 15 to 20 years of production, followed by another 15 years of continuing application of the last aircraft produced). During that time, as we have seen, the aircraft company may have invested $4 to $6 billion (exclusive of engine development) and have waited 10 to 15 years or more before it recovers the investment--even for successful aircraft (Figure 2-11).

Evidence on the profitability of individual jet transport families such as the B707 or the DC-9 is not entirely consistent. One author having intimate contact with the industry states that out of 22 commercial jet aircraft developed, only 2--the Boeing 707 and 727--have been profitable.[13] (The widely regarded <u>Economist</u> adds the DC-8 to the list.[14]) All others have been unprofitable. One must assume, however, that a number of the U.S. programs may have achieved sizable positive cash flows at times during their production that were critical to company reinvestment needs for successive rounds of new product developments; otherwise, the U.S. civil industry would reflect a different history. During this period U.S. manufacturers dominated a world market that was growing vibrantly. The modest financial performance of the past suggests there could be serious problems addressing future competitive opportunities. In addition to the changes in markets and international competition noted above, the manufacturers are increasingly exposed to additional risk because of the necessity to participate in financing the sale of aircraft--a subject that will be discussed later. One cannot envy aircraft manufacturers this financial and management challenge.

MANAGEMENT CHALLENGES

The changes occurring in the environment pose major challenges to the management of civil aircraft manufacturing. This environment can be summarized as follows: Projections of market requirements--always precarious--are even more so with the structure and performance of U.S. airlines in turmoil and foreign markets looming as increasingly important in the future. The investment required to launch new aircraft incorporating new technology is escalating. With the life cycle of the first commercial jet transports drawing to a close, one can begin to assess their impact on the investment attractiveness of the aircraft manufacturers, and the results are modest.

The deteriorating balance sheets and uncertain future of domestic airlines are leading to increasing caution by the conventional providers of financing for new aircraft; they are becoming more cautious in providing additional funds. Consequently, manufacturers themselves are finding it necessary to participate in financing sales of aircraft and thus to enlarge their own exposure and increase their own requirements to raise capital.

After only limited success in 30 years of trying, the Europeans now have presented to the world market a large transport that is technologically sound and commercially viable. While one cannot predict the future, it is unlikely that with this budding success the Europeans will continue to accept a U.S. monopoly in large transports. The A300 provides the entry on which Airbus can build. In addition, Japan has now announced its intention to become a significant participant in aerospace industry.

In the face of this array, U.S. manufacturers also possess formidable strengths: a decades-long record of producing technologically advanced, cost-effective aircraft that meet customer needs; a global capability for service; massive investment in modern facilities; an infrastructure that in fact supports aircraft manufacture globally; and technological leadership that, while admittedly narrowing and vulnerable, still exists.[15]

Among the many challenges with which manufacturers must contend the following warrant special mention:

1. Accommodating the increasing cost associated with validating and introducing new technology in the face of a historical record of modest financial results is a major challenge. The trend toward managing escalating financial risk by moving toward incremental improvements in technology and incorporating them gradually through derivatives is a rational response. The skill demonstrated in this initial phase of managing technology will play a major role in determining the future success of aircraft manufacturers.

2. Participating in financing aircraft sales will in many cases determine whether a sale can be made. The ingenuity now being displayed in this arena has opened a new dimension in competition; the size, sophistication, and flexibility of the U.S. capital market and its long time scale are important competitive resources that are being exploited through new financial instruments and arrangements. These efforts inevitably include deeper involvement in the sale of secondhand aircraft and increase the risk of serious loss. Special attention needs to be paid to the development of new financial instruments and mechanisms that will spread this risk.

3. Perhaps the biggest challenge is also the most subtle--moving from a position of overwhelming global dominance to senior partnership with manufacturers in other countries. With clear evidence of progress in intra-European cooperation and potential market success in sight, the Europeans are unlikely to abandon their 30-year effort to participate in large transports. The emergence of likely Japanese participation broadens this competition and makes it more threatening. U.S. manufacturers have already begun to respond--continued confrontation across the board does not appear attractive. Steps toward interdependence will require learning how to work effectively in a partnership mode--and some Europeans are saying they will make more effective partners with the Japanese than will the powerful U.S. firms. Subtle problems of balancing domestic employment versus access to foreign markets and of preserving technological leadership while cooperating in technology development must also be faced.

4. Accommodating to the likelihood that the United States will no longer be able to maintain leadership in every aeronautical design and production technology and ensuring leadership in those technologies critical for preserving competitive advantage are additional challenges. Many governments in developed and

developing countries have identified their civil aviation sectors for special support. These governments recognize that establishing a technology base in design and production is a mandatory concomitant of achieving commercial viability, and they will do whatever is necessary to create that base. The growing importance of international markets increases the likelihood that control of access to markets will be used as a lever for increasing participation in manufacture. The comparative technological position of foreign firms will almost inevitably improve. Consequently, it is no longer realistic to assume that leadership in virtually all aspects of aircraft design and manufacture--which the United States enjoyed for many years--will continue to be sustainable. Internationalization of manufacture may well continue to grow, and the United States must recognize and accept the likelihood of foreign parity or leadership in some aspects of aircraft technology development and production.

Preserving the viability of the U.S. companies capable of being systems integrators in developing, designing, manufacturing, and selling new aircraft is the key to preserving the critical mass of the infrastructure required for national security and for competitive leadership. Thus, initiating the actions that will retain the United States' overall technological leadership in a matrix of international cooperation requires special attention. It is important for the managers of the civil aircraft industry and of the supporting industrial substructure to determine those aspects of development, design, and production that are critical to maintaining competitive leadership. They must then allocate resources selectively to achieve that objective. How these choices evolve is a matter of private and public concern warranting careful attention.

Exercising this kind of selectivity is complex and frequently involves painful choices, but in the face of the emerging international competition it cannot be avoided. Managing international interdependence in technology in a way that preserves overall leadership will call for vision and wisdom by U.S. managers in an arena in which they have had relatively little experience.

PRESERVING HUMAN RESOURCES

Civil aircraft manufacture demonstrates in extreme form the characteristics of a cyclical industry with high labor content. Abrupt variations in equipment purchases by both DOD and the airlines exacerbate the changes in volume. This characteristic of the industry imposes especially severe employment uncertainty on the skilled workers who design, test, and produce sophisticated modern aircraft. Technological obsolescence creates an additional element of uncertainty for the work force. For example, the introduction of new materials and processes, new production and assembly technologies, and methods of testing and quality control often generate a requirement for radically different skills. In the past the U.S. industry has responded to such change or cyclical fluctuations in orders by hiring or laying off production workers, engineers, and managers in pace with need. Foreign industries, constrained by laws and social practices, have tended to avoid expanding employment to meet demand peaks, have subsidized employment at low demand, and have in some cases resisted pressures for technical change that would increase productivity.

Fortunately, U.S. workers and labor unions in the industry have long recognized the vital role of new technology in maintaining the health of this industry. In the heightened competitive climate of the aviation industry it is exceedingly important for management and workers and their union representatives to strengthen the dialogue on the introduction of new technology. Worker concerns over displacement, loss of income, and erosion of skills, if not adequately addressed and if blamed on technology, can turn into resistance to change that would be detrimental to the competitive position of the industry. The growing awareness of the important contribution that workers can make to improved productivity and quality, when they feel that they have truly participated in the process of technological innovation, represents a powerful opportunity for the industry to strengthen its competitive position.

The assemblage of human skills and working team relationships in the aircraft manufacturing industry represent a priceless and irreplaceable national resource. A deterioration in financial performance or a long gap in the development and launch of new aircraft would seriously threaten the survival of these teams. If they were dispersed, the loss would be severe--possibly irretrievable.

The United States has not yet developed adequate mechanisms with which to dampen cyclical unemployment. Furthermore, the social and economic costs such unemployment generates are neither adequately quantified nor incorporated into the calculation of the economic contribution and performance of the industry. The fact that the timing of procurement for defense also makes no allowance for employment stability only exacerbates the problem. This is much less true in other countries. It is apparent that a major consideration in the drive of other governments to establish an indigenous aviation industry is the attractive employment level and skill content associated with aircraft manufacture. They also recognize the synergism between civil and military aviation. Such governments give high priority to employment stability, and they calculate the full social and economic costs of unemployment when negotiating sales and trade agreements. These costs, in fact, become a factor in setting prices, terms, and conditions for sale of aircraft. The goal is to achieve a more nearly level production rate and increased production efficiencies for these foreign manufacturers. If foreign manufacturers deliberately limited their market penetration to a level compatible with stable employment (a not unlikely scenario), U.S. manufacturers would be left to accommodate the even more cyclical portion that remained. U.S. manufacturers, no matter what they might wish, lack the resources to stabilize their production rate. Nor are they responsible for, or in a position to reap fully, the associated social and economic benefits that accrue to the nation from more stable employment.

Some panel members believe that the mechanisms that other countries have established to ameliorate employment instability have imposed increased rigidity on their operations, reduced the ability of management to respond rapidly to changing competitive circumstances, and in turn resulted in restraints on technological innovation in the workplace. They fear that these stabilizing mechanisms would have the same inhibiting effect on the United States. Consequently, the desire of U.S. industry to maintain technological momentum and to avoid these disadvantages suggests the need to search for solutions less penalizing than the political and economic solutions being used in other countries. Other panel members, however, suggest that increased employment stability creates a more favorable environment for technological innovation in the workplace, and that the social and economic benefits of employment-stabilizing policies more than offset the costs of any increased operating rigidities. Among the problems that need urgent attention are:

• Retirement security--Due to the large variations in employment, workers can complete an entire career in aircraft manufacture and never accumulate enough time with one employer to qualify for an adequate pension. It is reasonable for management, workers, and government to give specific attention to the development and implementation of policies and programs that allow workers to accrue retirement benefits commensurate with their employment experience, not just their attachments to individual employers.

• Unemployment--It is a responsibility of management, workers, and government to develop instruments that minimize employment instability and ameliorate, insofar as possible, the costs of periodic job loss, a condition that has been characteristic of the industry. The "migrant" skilled worker phenomenon has not yet been adequately addressed.

• Training—The high rate of technological change in both the product and workplace that characterizes the industry imposes a special requirement that there be mechanisms allowing workers to develop new skills and to share equitably in the fruits of technology.

It is believed that resolution of these issues will promote the flexibility and efficiency of the industry, advance its ability to maintain a competitive lead in the incorporation of new technologies, and allocate costs and benefits more fairly across the industry and the economy.

NOTES

1. E.L. Thomas, "Deregulated—ATA Maintenance and Engineering," Air Transport Association of America, presentation at 1981 ATA Engineering and Maintenance Forum, San Diego, Cal., October 27-29, 1981.

2. D. W. Caves, Laurits R. Christensen, Michael W. Threthway, "Productivity Performance of U.S. Trunk and Local Service Airlines in the Era of Deregulation," Economic Inquiry, Vol. XV, Number 3, July 1983, pp. 312-324.

3. New York Times Magazine, February 19, 1984, pp. 42-55.

4. Paul R. Ignatius, Air Transport Association of America, statement before the Aviation Subcommittee on Public Works and Transportation Committee, U.S. House of Representatives, May 24, 1983.

5. Airline Executive, November 1983, pp. 39, 40.

6. Aerospace Research Center. The Challenge of Foreign Competition, Foreign Competition Project Group, Commercial Transport Aircraft Committee, Aerospace Industries Association of America, March 1976.

7. Garret Turbine Engine Co., based partly on article in Financial Times of Canada, October 6, 1980.

8. (a) United States Trade Council, Japan's Aircraft Industry, Washington, D.C., January 11, 1980.

(b) Ministry of International Trade and Industry, The Vision of MITI Policies in 1980s, Tokyo, Ministry of International Trade and Industry, March 17, 1980.

(c) "Technology and Environment—MITI Plans Development of New Aeronautical Technology," The Japan Economic Journal, June 10, 1980.

(d) Report to the Chairman, Joint Economic Committee, United States Congress, "Industrial Policy: Case Studies in the Japanese Experience," GAO, October 20, 1982.

(e) <u>Japanese Industrial Policies and the Development of High Technology Industries, Computers and Aircraft,</u> U.S. Department of Commerce, International Trade Administration, February 1983, pg. 39.

(f) <u>Japan Air Transport Handbook,</u> May 1981, pg. 91.

9. The CF6 series (or P&W JT9D series) engines are used. The CF-6-50 is a GE-designed engine that is produced jointly by GE, SNECMA, and MTU of West Germany for the A300 application. GE produces about two-thirds of the engines and SNECMA and MTU the rest.

10. From conversations of Lowell W. Steele with British aviation representatives, February 1983.

11. Transcript of documentary program "The Fifth Estate-- Canadair" produced and shown by Canadian Broadcasting Company, April 14, 1983.

12. From conversations of Lowell W. Steele with repre- sentatives of Airbus Industrie in Great Britain, France, and West Germany.

13. John Newhouse, "A Reporter at Large. A Sporty Game III: Big, Bigger, Jumbo." <u>The New Yorker,</u> June 28, 1982, p. 58.

14. "Aerospace Survey," <u>The Economist,</u> August 30, 1980, pp. 5-22.

15. The impact of current U.S. antitrust statutes and practices regarding technological innovation and product development in the aircraft industry was a topic of recurrent discussion by panel members. However, the panel did not develop a sense of priority regarding the urgency of this subject nor did it reach a consensus concerning the desirability of revisions in the statutes and enforcement guidelines.

3

Growing Government Involvement in Trade

IMPACT OF GOVERNMENT INVOLVEMENT

As mentioned repeatedly, throughout the post-World War II era foreign governments have been heavily involved in supporting the development, production, marketing, and sale of aircraft as well as in the operation of a largely government-owned air transport system.[1] This involvement has covered the spectrum from mandating aircraft specifications to meet specific national airline requirements (as in the case of government-owned British European Airways in specifying the design of the Trident), to funding development (as in the case of the Conway engine, the Caravelle, Concorde, and A300 aircraft), to financing uneconomically low rates of production (for the RB-211, A300, A310, and other aircraft).[2]

Foreign government support, through its ownership of or involvement in the industry, has also been directed at regional transports such as the C-212, the helicopter family of Aerospatiale, the Canadair Challenger, the British BAe146, the Bandeirante of Brazil, and the CN235 developed jointly by Nuritania of Indonesia and CASA of Spain.

This support was provided for a variety of reasons, as has been noted, e.g., to sustain an indigenous industry, to avoid a condition of dependency, to provide employment, to stimulate technical growth, and to foster national prestige. The limited commercial success of such foreign aircraft through the 1970s minimized the competitive impact on the U.S. aircraft industry. On balance, the programs probably constituted a net drain to the economies of the countries involved. Such calculations are not easily made, however, in part because assumptions must be made about the level of unemployment if the program had not been sponsored, about the social and economic costs of unemployment and about the value or loss of value of the spread of technology to other industries.

75

There can be no doubt that government involvement changes the competitive equation significantly. Not only is the calculation of costs and benefits based on broader and more diffuse criteria than is possible for a private company, but also the time periods for judging results and seeking payback are much longer. For example, Airbus A300 production began in 1972, but when deliveries began in 1977 there was only a total of 10 firm orders.

Furthermore, the terms specifying timing and conditions of payback are often more indeterminate than is possible with a conventional private financial arrangement.[3] The production of the A300 and A310 for inventory, begun during the 1981-1982 recession, is still continuing. No private enterprise could, or would, propose these actions. The production for inventory provides a marked delivery advantage as a market recovers. It also provides a powerful incentive to offer below-market terms and conditions for sales financing in order to move the aircraft out of inventory. Both faster delivery and attractive financing have obvious competitive advantages.

Another way in which government involvement affects the competitive situation is in its capacity to sustain a program over long time periods. For example, only 180 Australian Nomads were sold in 18 years. The Europeans have been seeking to establish a viable civil aircraft industry for almost 30 years, and to a degree they are now beginning to succeed. In 1980 Japan's Ministry of International Trade and Industry (MITI) identified aerospace as one of Japan's future industries, and the building of a capability for its aerospace technologies as one of the two most important things for the industry's future (see Note 8, Chapter 3). This and MITI's announced plans for Japan's aircraft sector to be competitive with Western industry by 2010 indicate the long time scale with which Japan's government approaches targeted industries. The common assumption among both U.S. and European aircraft manufacturers is that Japan intends to play a major role sometime in the mid-1990s and beyond and to use international joint development programs as an avenue to build competence. Indeed, the long time intervals for design and development and the long aircraft lifetimes are well matched to the long time horizon that can characterize government initiatives.

The airline procurement process has always been politicized. It is instructive to note that British Airways, Air France, and Air Inter (a domestic French airline) were required to purchase the BAC-111, the Trident, and the Caravelle as long as they were in production. More recently, the Airbus A300 and A310 have benefited from this directed mode of procurement in France.

Involvement by the French government was evident in the engine procurement decision for the Air France Airbus A310 during the last half of 1979.[4] The General Electric-SNECMA

(U.S.-French) partnership[5] was competing vigorously with Pratt and Whitney. The specific engine involved was a version of the CF6, but GE and SNECMA had an extensive history of coproduction of engines and were also currently partners in developing a new engine, the CFM 56. Which engine Air France should be allowed to purchase was the subject of debate between ministries of the French government and was the subject of two formal interministerial reviews. The government finally directed purchase of the GE/SNECMA engine, with its partial French content. This example not only demonstrates the impact of government involvement but also the advantage of an international partnership for a U.S. manufacturer.

The trends in air transport noted earlier, which forecast more rapid growth for the developing countries, amplify the significance of government involvement in future marketing and sales. Since most airlines in these countries are nationally owned and aircraft procurements represent major expenses, the procurements are subject to review at ministerial levels. Inevitably, the process is politicized. With Airbus looming as a major competitor, the opportunity is growing for purchasing decisions to be made, as they have been, through government-to-government negotiations.

Situations in which a foreign government is involved in negotiations are frequently subject to widespread allegations of offers of tie-in sales, technology assistance in other fields, and counter-trade proposals that a private firm cannot match. The belief is widespread in industry that these inducements are frequently used and are effective. Not surprisingly, no documented evidence of such arrangements is available. The experience of U.S. government administrators who monitor activities in this field is that such actions are sometimes attempted, but in fact rarely work and can be countered by candid discussion. On occasion the pressure generated by zealous government support has been counterproductive. These somewhat differing points of view undoubtedly reflect the different channels of information that are available to each group.

IMPLICATIONS FOR INTERNATIONAL TRADE AGREEMENTS

The Agreement on Trade in Civil Aircraft, effective January 1, 1980, concluded under the General Agreement on Tariffs and Trade (GATT) as part of the Tokyo Round, is one of several multilateral agreements intended to control and monitor government subsidies and other trade practices affecting civil aircraft sales. This agreement requires the abolition of all customs duties on trade in aircraft and many of their components, the avoidance of government pressure on parties to procurement transactions, and requires that "civil aircraft prices should be based on a reasonable expectation of recoupment of all costs."

The agreement has facilitated trade in aircraft components, but is neutral to the internationalization of the industry through joint ventures and licensing. Although practice varies among countries, the experience of U.S. trade administrators and U.S. industry is that the agreement is useful. For example, both Great Britain and West Germany are thought to exact conditions for lending and repayment that are somewhat comparable to those that would be required by private financiers.

The issue of subsidy is exceedingly complex. In virtually every developed country, including the United States, intimate relationships between government and aircraft manufacturing have existed for decades. The relationship covers every aspect of the industry from research to manufacturing facilities to sales financing. Modes of support are diverse and obscured by the passage of time. Opportunities for argument abound on every detail that may be under negotiation regarding a particular sale and legitimate costs for the pricing of a product. Consequently, one must have modest expectations regarding attainable progress in trade discussions to assure compliance with agreements. One must keep in mind that the U.S. objective is not to eliminate subsidies (an unrealistic goal), but rather to eliminate trade-distorting subsidies such as selling below cost.[6] The fact remains that negotiations related to previously agreed trade standards represent the only vehicle currently accepted by our trading partners. The United States has little choice except to pursue trade negotiations as vigorously as possible, recognizing their limitations. To do otherwise invites trade wars with implications and ramifications that are difficult to predict, much less control.

The aircraft industry suffers from two special vulnerabilities connected with the ex post facto monitoring of compliance with international trade agreements: the large size of individual aircraft purchases and the leverage gained by initial sales. Aircraft purchases tend to come in spurts rather than in a continuous flow as an airline replaces aging equipment or adds capacity. Consequently, by the time the terms of a transaction have been determined to be in violation of a trade agreement the entire sales opportunity can be over. The importance of this circumstance is magnified by the leverage of initial orders. Airlines prefer commonality of equipment for better logistics in stocking parts and for greater efficiency in the operation of flight and maintenance crews. Consequently, the manufacturer who secures the initial order has a major advantage with respect to all subsequent orders.

While various provisions of the Agreement on Trade in Civil Aircraft have been questioned, the agreement does provide a forum for discussion on trade policy issues that can prevent the occurrence of or help resolve a dispute before it escalates. It also strengthens the basis for demonstrating injury and pursuing countervailing duties and other actions within the United States.

The agreement is weakened to a degree by its failure to include all of the nations involved in aircraft production. Brazil, Israel, Spain, Indonesia, and Australia are not signatories. There is some reason to believe that their reluctance to sign reflects a desire to change their competitive position in the world market. Spain will be brought under the terms of the agreement should it join the EEC. The agreement's enforcement on a "most-favored nation" basis, however, means that signatory and nonsignatory nations are treated equally by signatories and thus nonsignatories have no incentive to join insofar as tariff protection is concerned. The "most-favored nation" treatment, however, does provide a basis for discussions with nonsignatories of their policy on import restrictions. Brazil, Israel, and Indonesia are protected by the agreement's tariff provisions in approaching the U.S. market, but the agreement is not binding on their governments with regard to sales in those countries. Enforcement of the agreement, though aggressively pursued, has been hampered to some degree in the past by insufficient data and staff resources.

Recent steps taken in the U.S. Department of Commerce to organize along the lines of industrial segments and to increase staff manyfold have dramatically strengthened the U.S. capability for monitoring and enforcement. U.S. administrative support is now comparable in an absolute sense with that in key European countries; however, elected officers at the highest level, the diplomatic corps, and even royalty are thought to be more actively involved in supporting trade than their counterparts in the United States. Furthermore, the aggregate participation of those countries in international trade in civil aircraft is small compared with its importance to U.S. trade. Unfortunately, our expanded effort is vulnerable to the political changes in administration.

The panel endorses the recent action to strengthen capability for monitoring and enforcement and recommends that the importance of this activity receive sufficiently broad political endorsement that it transcends changes in administration.

The panel recommends continuing vigorous efforts by the United States to bring into the Agreement on Trade in Civil Aircraft those nonsignatory countries currently or prospectively exporting to the United States.

One might argue that this effort could be facilitated by the possible revocation of "most-favored nation" status for nonsignatory countries, a basic principle of GATT. Such a step obviously should be taken only after active negotiation to induce nonsignators to join indicates the futility of other measures and with careful consideration of the consequences. It chief value would be as a threat.

The panel also recommends more vigorous data collection, monitoring, assessment, and enforcement of the GATT agreement by government personnel for all segments of the aircraft industry, not just large commercial jets.

Enforcement could be facilitated by a higher degree of coordination among the U.S. agencies most directly involved in implementation--the United States Trade Representative's office, the Department of Commerce, the Department of State--and those agencies responsible for related, and frequently conflicting, policies--the Department of State, the Department of Defense, and the National Security Council.

Providing More Flexible and Timely Response

Foreign support of R&D, risk capital, and export finance are indicative of a larger policy issue, namely, the desire of foreign governments to support the development of an indigenous aircraft industry using economic criteria that are not applicable to private firms in the United States. Agreements aimed at controlling government subsidization of indigenous industries inevitably can be evaded, given a political will to do so. However, the U.S. government should continue to pursue such agreements for the reasons that have been indicated. Nonetheless, in the final analysis, it may be necessary to develop U.S. policies that recognize the "targeting" of the civil aircraft industry by foreign governments and that reflect the broad national security, economic, and social interests served by a healthy U.S. aircraft manufacturing industry. Said another way, it is desirable to recognize that economic and social interests are important dimensions of national security along with the obvious dimension of military strength.

The transitory nature of many of the most flagrant foreign-government trade policies and the problems of large individual orders and first-sale leverage, noted earlier, suggest the importance of timeliness and the need for a variety of potential responses in formulating and administering U.S. trade policy--responses that can vary in strength, in length, and in the nature of their administrative implementation. Options could include much closer coordination of U.S. military development and procurement practices with industrial need, tighter and more extensive integration of NASA with civil R&D, as well as more aggressive U.S. export finance policies.

One area of action that should be explored in response to flagrant distortion of trade agreements by foreign governments is the possible utility of retaliatory measures that are clearly temporary. Temporary measures that permit immediate unilateral action could expire in six months or less, barring certification of continued subsidization of sales or other forms of predatory action by foreign governments. Examples of such temporary policies include the denial of investment tax credit on the foreign-produced (non-U.S. labor) content of imported aircraft, or the prohibition of loans under the FAA loan guarantee program for purchases of foreign aircraft with a U.S. content below some threshold (e.g., 35 percent). Such retaliatory measures are not without danger, because they in turn invite retaliation, not necessarily in the field in question, but rather where the foreign government feels it has the greatest leverage. Their existence on a standby basis, however, would be a clear signal of the importance attached to the problem and would add another dimension to the options available to our trade negotiators. Foreign trade negotiations are like a high-stakes poker game, and it is important for our negotiators to have as potent a list of bargaining ploys as do their counterparts.

Temporary measures could, in principle, be invoked on short notice and could thus help alleviate the problems of slowness of response. As noted earlier, the pace of commercial negotiations and the ebb and flow of competitive success in the marketplace are frequently faster than the ability to mobilize the machinery of government and to generate a response. Improvement requires action by both industry and government. In the past, there have been painful occasions when by the time some members of the industry recognized the need to invoke government participation, learned to deal with the bureaucracy, and built a case that would initiate government action, and appropriate government agencies had coordinated their positions, the transaction had already been completed. The recent changes in the U.S. Department of Commerce provide the basis for more timely government action. Recognition of these changes is not yet widespread in industry. Both trade associations and government must be active in fostering improvement. Government can be most useful when it is involved early and can initiate discussions with other governments before bargaining ploys have surfaced and positions have become more intractable.

FINANCING

A particularly troubling aspect of government involvement concerns financing of purchases. Due to the large sums of money and the long time interval associated with payback, financing terms have significant leverage on the eventual cost to the customer. The discussion that follows will examine the general situation and then look specifically at the circumstances for large aircraft and smaller aircraft. Export credit and export subsidies are a common feature of foreign trade and a topic on which Organization for Economic Cooperation and Development (OECD) negotiations were conducted in 1975. The agreement was intended to cover all capital goods, but Great Britain, France, West Germany, and the United States were unable to reach agreement on civil aircraft--an indication of the resolve of others to alter the competitive picture in aircraft. Consequently, a so-called "standstill" was adopted under which the OECD nations agreed not to offer in the future terms more favorable than then being offered.

The 1975 "standstill" set a maximum of 10 years on the repayment period for loans to purchase large transport aircraft, but 12 years for leases. However, it set no minimum for interest rates. The limitation on the term of the repayment period does not coincide with the useful life of aircraft (20 to 25 years); furthermore, it abrogates a powerful U.S. competitive weapon, the strong long-term (20 to 30 years) capital market, a feature lacking in Europe. This short period in itself constitutes a barrier to sales because it mandates a rapid repayment schedule that necessitates large early payments.

As market interest rates began to escalate, the United States found itself in an increasingly disadvantageous position. The absence of a minimum for interest rates offered opportunities for increasing levels of subsidy through lower-than-market interest rates--a condition the agreement was intended to bring under control. Airbus made aggressive use of such interest subsidies in its marketing.

As interest rates escalated further, the United States undertook to negotiate a "commonline" with the Airbus-financing governments. We succeeded in establishing a minimum interest (eventually 12 percent on U.S. dollar loans) that was still below market rates, with the repayment period remaining at 10 years.

Agreements in export finance are no stronger than the political will of their signatory governments. However, these agreements clarify and ratify the basis for retaliatory actions, and they provide a forum for continuing multilateral and bilateral negotiations over trade policy.

The panel endorses and recommends continued vigorous efforts to eliminate all forms of trade-distorting mechanisms[7] so that normal market forces can operate effectively.

Large Aircraft

The Export-Import Bank (Eximbank), as part of the "common-line" agreement relating to large transport aircraft, charges a fixed rate of 12 percent plus a 0.5 percent commitment fee. However, it charges a 2 percent application fee that is paid either up front or over the first six semiannual installments. This procedure raises the effective rate to 12.5 percent. On the guarantee option, the guarantee fee is 0.5 percent with no loan application fee. However, the funding of the guaranteed paper is at market rates.[8]

The European export agencies only provide credit guarantees, but will support aircraft exports to the extent of 62.5 percent of the cost of the aircraft rather than 42.5 percent as in the case of the Eximbank. In consequence the U.S. has offered 62.5 percent and the Europeans have come down to 42.5 percent on recent competitive transactions. Eximbank repayment occurs only after private lenders have been repaid. The funds are provided by private institutions, but the export agencies subsidize the rate at the commonline level, which is presently 12 percent. Both the Eximbank and the European agencies will provide financing up to 85 percent if the other offers it.

The basic result is that the direct financing of a sale is close to parity except for the 2 percent application fee (the normal European fee is 0.3 percent). This fee makes the financing of the U.S. export more expensive and is particularly onerous because it represents an "up front" payment from airlines that frequently are scrambling to raise the down payment on the aircraft. The market rate for the Eximbank guarantee of 85 percent of the cost is balanced against the subsidized interest rate on up to 62.5 percent financing by the Europeans with the balance of 27.5 percent at market rate. However, in cases where the Europeans go up to 85 percent with a subsidized rate, the Eximbank guarantee program is more expensive, particularly when the 0.5 percent commitment fee is included.

Although the commonline agreement that relates to large transport aircraft calls for a 10-year term, both Eximbank and the European agencies are willing to guarantee a 12-year lease transaction. However, a 12-year term and the requirement of equal semiannual payments of principal damage the economics of a tax lease. The optimal time period of a tax lease is 15 to 18 years.

Another competitive problem for the U.S. manufacturers relates to the practice of the European manufacturers to fund their exports in their own currencies. Under the terms of commonline agreements, the European export credit agencies may lend German marks at 9.5 percent and French francs at 11.5 percent, while U.S. dollar loans are at 12 percent. In competitions over the last several years it has become very clear that not all airlines regard these rates in the various currencies as equivalent. The U.S. Eximbank will lend only dollars but allows its guarantee to be used to raise loans in other currencies. This latter option does not match the European offers because commercial banks cannot offer to fix an interest rate 18 to 24 months in advance of aircraft delivery and, in any case, will lend only at commercial rates. The French franc rate has been highly subsidized during the entire existence of the commonline agreement. The only solution that completely neutralizes this issue is for Eximbank to offer to lend directly at commonline rates not only U.S. dollars but also German marks and French francs.

United States exporters are adversely affected by Eximbank policy with respect to airlines of developing countries. The Eximbank charter requires "a reasonable assurance of repayment," which is often used to turn down loan applications from airlines of developing countries. In contrast, the European export agencies are more liberal. It should also be noted that the "commonline" agreement does not cover exports of Fokker and British Aerospace to developing countries. However, on such transactions, the commonline agreement on interest cost is adhered to on 85 to 95 percent of the transactions.

Another disadvantage for U.S. manufacturers is that the Eximbank will not cover the foreign content of a U.S. export while the European export agencies will. In consequence, the U.S. exporter has to find another way to finance this portion of the aircraft cost. With growing percentage of foreign content in U.S. aircraft exports, this becomes an increasing problem and a competitive disadvantage for the U.S. manufacturers.

The Eximbank and the European agencies now have an informal understanding not to provide financing commitments in one another's countries, i.e., the United Kingdom, France, West Germany, and the United States. This recent development can prevent some of the unusual transactions conducted in the past.

Unfortunately, the Eximbank has been inconsistent over the years not only in its policy toward large aircraft exports but also in administering that policy. This has inhibited the ability of customers to plan their equipment purchases and related financing. In dealing with the European agencies they knew where they stood. Although Eximbank will meet foreign competition, it is often unwilling to provide financing where no competition exists. This policy limits sales to some customers, particularly to developing countries where alternative sources of funds are not available. More disturbing is the policy of Eximbank to insist on a competitive offer from a foreign manufacturer before it will agree to finance a U.S. aircraft export. This can have the effect of requiring the aircraft manufacturers to induce competition when none may otherwise have existed.

As can be seen, the Eximbank export support for large transports falls short of meeting foreign competitive financing. In consequence, the burden has fallen on the manufacturer to provide competitive financing. Competitive pressures in financing international sales have combined with an uncertain earnings outlook and cash flow difficulties to stimulate new forms of financing. Many carriers and their lenders have become hesitant to take on substantial long-term debt service commitments for new aircraft. Ironically, the success of an industry that has historically been a bellwether of technological innovation is increasingly dependent on innovation in financial instruments and arrangements.

Some recent transactions for both domestic and international carriers have been based on an operating-lease concept in which the airline commits itself to lease aircraft for a two- or three-year lease payment term. The concept involves structuring the transaction as a tax lease with the lessor taking the investment tax credit and the accelerated depreciation. This then reduces the lease payments. The balance of the cost is raised from banks, institutional lenders, or the public market.

The problem associated with such operating leases is that should the airline return the aircraft at the end of the initial lease term, the senior lenders would have considerable exposure against the residual value of the aircraft, and the equity investor would be in danger of losing the tax benefits if the aircraft could not be leased again. As a result, some mechanism must be devised that would make such a transaction, with its residual risk implications, attractive to both equity investors and senior lenders.

In spite of the inadequacy of airline operating profits to pay for "new generation" aircraft, manufacturers have been under considerable pressure to get their aircraft in the hands of carriers that represent good potential for follow-on orders, particularly when the alternative would be to close down the aircraft manufacturing line. Not surprisingly, many recent transactions have involved substantial manufacturer financing.

Senior lenders could probably be induced to take an asset risk in the range of 50 to 60 percent of the aircraft price, provided the manufacturer were willing to assume the responsibility of remarketing the aircraft in the event of a default by the airline. Unfortunately, banks are limited to a 25 percent asset risk on an operating lease. It might be possible to secure residual value insurance for a portion of the asset risk. However, the market for residual value insurance is thin, and the volume of the risk that can be covered in this manner is uncertain. Consequently, it is not clear that a large number of aircraft could be financed on this basis, because of the problems outlined. In addition, the expense of the insurance can adversely affect the economics of the transaction.

Another possible approach that might reduce the residual risk is to develop a special entity to purchase aircraft and enter into operating leases with a number of airlines. The risk would be spread over time and over a large number of borrowers since not every airline would turn back aircraft at the end of the initial lease period.

The financial community, the aircraft manufacturers, and the airlines need to continue efforts to design financing packages that meet airline minimal cash flow and balance sheet requirements and that minimize the exposure of the manufacturers while assisting them in making sales. The panel recognizes that use of tax policy to improve international competitiveness is controversial, largely because it involves tax "expenditure" to encourage exports. Those exports do, however, represent business that otherwise would not exist and thus enlarge the tax base. Nevertheless, government tax policies obviously will continue to play a critical role in determining the attractiveness of such arrangements.

The panel recommends consideration of additional measures that would enable aircraft manufacturers to reduce the risk in leasing aircraft to domestic and foreign customers. Many of these steps would involve removal of legal roadblocks rather than increased financial exposure for the government.

Unlike banks or other financial entities that are currently or prospectively engaged in such leasing (e.g., insurance companies), aircraft firms engaging in leasing do not hold highly diversified or liquid portfolios of financial assets or have a broad customer base compared with financial institutions. Therefore, large transport and especially commuter aircraft producers face greater risk of catastrophic financial losses than more diversified lessors. The ability of U.S. aircraft producers to finance new products in the deregulated airline environment would be enhanced if restrictions that determine a "true" lease (i.e., one that allows five-year depreciation) and the claiming of the investment tax credit on the part of the lessor were liberalized. Easing restrictions would partially equalize the financial risks faced by lending institutions and aircraft producers in leasing and allow aircraft demand to be exercised.

Leases of aircraft to foreign operators also have increased in recent years. However, current tax policy penalizes leases to foreign customers by restricting the eligibility for investment tax credit (ITC). Actions that would eliminate ITC for all non-U.S. aircraft operators would be counterproductive to this country's efforts to sell aircraft to non-U.S. operators. Continuing the use of tax leasing to the international airline community is an important marketing tool. An additional step that would be useful in enhancing sales to developing countries would be to include aircraft as infrastructure project equipment that qualifies for Agency for International Development (AID) and World Bank funding.

In view of the fact that over 60 percent of the current civil transport aircraft market is outside the United States, the availability of the investment tax credit to foreign operators will have a major and beneficial impact on the market for U.S. aircraft. Determining the net benefit or cost will require careful analysis.

The importance of foreign markets for the U.S. civil aircraft manufacturing industry means that congressional proposals to deny even the current, restrictively defined investment tax credit to foreign operators could have a serious and detrimental impact on the industry. However, as noted earlier, the denial of the investment tax credit on foreign aircraft purchases could serve a useful purpose as a temporary measure to countervail unfair trade practices. The earlier admonitions with respect to the dangers of invoking retaliatory measures must be repeated.

Recent changes in legislation have been enacted to improve the utility of special corporations to permit deferral of U.S. taxes on foreign sales. The rules governing the corporations (formerly called Domestic International Sales Corporations [DISCs], but now called Foreign Sales Corporations [FSCs]) have been modified to bring them into conformance with GATT. In the new legislation changes have been made that reduce the obligation for demonstrating a foreign presence for smaller firms, and they all provide for partial exemption of taxes rather than partial deferral, as formerly permitted. These changes can be of benefit to smaller enterprises in the civil aircraft industry in their efforts to expand export sales.

The panel recognizes that the subject of providing government support for financing export sales of aircraft is controversial (the same could be said for other long-lived capital goods that require large expenditures, e.g., electrical generating equipment). Opponents assert that the support benefits a few large companies--an assertion that ignores the benefit to the 15,000 enterprises that supply materials, components, and subsystems to the major designers and assemblers of aircraft. Opponents also assert that competitive markets should be allowed to work and question why American taxpayers should be asked to support foreigners who buy U.S. aircraft. To the first the panel responds that it is unrealistic to regard the international market for aircraft as "competitive" in the classical sense employed in economics. As this report has indicated, many countries--large and small, highly developed and developing--have explicitly targeted aircraft manufacture as an industry in which to participate. Financing is an area in which competitive advantage can be established much more easily than in technical superiority, better product planning, or better service. Private firms face abnormal forces when they attempt to compete in such a market. In an era in which balance of payments looms as a problem of major and continuing concern, it is important for government policy to recognize the realities of the international market in which a major source of exports operates.

Small Aircraft

In the case of small aircraft the impact of financing terms can be so large that it changes the competitive balance in the purchase of aircraft and can induce an airline to purchase foreign equipment. In some cases, if there were no access to very attractive terms, no equipment would be purchased at all. The preferential financing terms being offered by some foreign export agencies and manufacturers include a minimal down payment, below-market interest rate, lengthy maturity, and deferral of the repayment of principal for a number of years. Some U.S. regional airlines, with balance sheets and income statements that would not permit raising funds in the private debt markets, are purchasing foreign aircraft with these below-market financing terms.

These arrangements are the equivalent of discounting. For example, increasing the repayment period from 7 to 19 years produces savings to the buyer equal to a discounted present value of 11 percent of the purchase price. Alternatively, offering an interest rate of 6 percent versus 12 percent provides a reduction equivalent to 16.7 percent of the purchase price at a given repayment interval. (Differentials of this magnitude have, in fact, been encountered.) These savings in cash have a significant effect on breakeven point and thus on the competitive position of an airline. Naturally, cash-limited airlines welcome such concessionary credit terms.

To meet this competition, the Eximbank now offers the Medium Term Credit Program for U.S. manufacturers seeking to export general aviation aircraft. This program is directed at exports of all products including aircraft, providing funds for loans with a term normally of seven years, where foreign competition can be demonstrated to be drawing on subsidized export credits. The program provides no help in meeting foreign competition in the domestic market. This program is especially important because, as noted earlier, the market potential for regional aircraft is growing dramatically. Since aircraft of these sizes are within the capability of a modest-sized economy (especially if it purchases sophisticated components from the

United States), a number of countries are competing in the marketplace--and offering attractive financing as part of the package, e.g., the United Kingdom, France, Brazil, and Indonesia. Under the Medium Term Credit Program the Eximbank makes a fixed interest-rate loan commitment to the U.S. bank financing the export sale by loaning its funds on a recourse basis. Eximbank lends up to 85 percent of the contract value, and the buyer must make a 15 percent cash payment.

Most transactions under this program do not exceed $5 million, but recently the Eximbank agreed to change this limit to $10 million. The term for this type of loan is generally seven years; however, exceptions have been made extending the term to 10 years.

Loan pricing (cost) is based on whether the purchaser's country is rated 1, 2, or 3 in order of increasing risk. At present, for a "1" country the interest rate would be 12.4 percent, plus the usual 0.5 percent commitment fee.

To qualify for this program the U.S. aircraft manufacturer must provide evidence of subsidized competition from a foreign manufacturer.

While the Eximbank has played a major role in support of the export of large transports, similar assistance for rotorcraft, business, and commuter aircraft exports has been less abundant and/or effective until the inauguration of the medium-term Eximbank facility.

Despite the limited participation in this program at this early date, the panel endorses the action, and recommends its continuation.

The Eximbank medium-term credit program has the potential to assist in exports of many industries, including those outside the aircraft industry, where the individual transactions tend to be modest in size. The panel believes that the Eximbank's operations and policies should give highest priority to supporting the ability of U.S. exporters to offer comparable financing. The fact that in the case of smaller transactions such actions would incur higher administrative burdens should not be used as a deterrent.

Predatory financing presents a dangerous problem for imports. Although presently prohibited by "informal" understandings, a more certain solution should be sought. Establishing the capability at Eximbank to match terms offered in the U.S. market is better than providing a penalty after the fact through countervailing duties. The latter does not restore to a U.S. bidder the opportunity to win a sale. Matching terms is not prohibited in the Eximbank charter, but it would require a major change in practice. The panel recognizes that use of such a capability should be approached with caution because it could invite domestic customers to stimulate foreign competition in order to obtain better financing. Nevertheless, the availability of this type of action would signal the United States' determination to deter predatory pricing in U.S. markets as well as in foreign markets.

It should be noted that although Eximbank represents an important source of financing for export sale of aircraft, it serves many other industries as well. Consequently, actions of the type suggested below have as their objective improving the effectiveness of Eximbank in serving all of industry. In much of capital goods the terms of financing become a powerful competitive weapon that can counteract both technological strength and manufacturing efficiency.

STRENGTHENING EXIMBANK'S ROLE

The panel recommends that Eximbank reexamine its mode of operation and lending roles in the light of the heightened international competition facing all of U.S. civil aviation as well as all U.S. industry. Eximbank plays a critical role in the aviation industry and should make efforts to improve its ability not only to remove impediments but to strengthen the competitive position of the industry. Examples include establishing a consistent policy toward exports to ensure customer confidence; eliminating the requirement for a competitive offer from a foreign manufacturer as a condition of Eximbank financing, permitting foreign content to be included in the financing packages, and extending the term of Eximbank--guaranteed financing from 10 to 15 years.

NOTES

1. Foreign Aeronautics Environment, NASA briefing data for Office of Science and Technology Policy, April 1983.
2. Thomas J. Bacher, Boeing Commercial Airplane Company, "The Economics of the Civil Aircraft Industry," Conference on The Role of Southeast Asia in World Airline and Aerospace Development, Singapore, September 24-25, 1981.
3. The Economist, March 3, 1984, p. 62.
4. (a) The Economist, October 13, 1979.
    (b) Aviation Magazine, January 7, 1980.
5. An informative account of this pioneering joint venture is available in Parker, Elbert C., "Foreign Transfer of Technology: A Case Study of the GE/SNECMA 10-Ton Engine Venture." A research report submitted to the faculty of the Air War College, Air University, Maxwell Air Force Base, Alabama, April 1974.

6. This fee is not required by the Commonline Agreement for Aircraft, an understanding reached by the export financing agencies of the United States, France, West Germany, and the United Kingdom. For other than OECD countries, Eximbank charges higher rates than for nonaircraft products.

7. The term trade-distorting mechanisms is simple in principle, but efforts to reduce it to a definition that can be applied in practice have proved to be difficult. The term refers to nontariff actions that would lead to market shares that differ from those that free market forces would create. With respect to aircraft the large leverage of financing has focused attention on efforts to remove financing as a factor that would influence the purchase decision. The goal of "market rate, market term" for interest and repayment is regarded as an important step that would be amenable to monitoring and evaluation. Even though this limited step would not address all aspects of trade distortion, its vigorous pursuit would be beneficial and consistent with the traditional position of the United States on free, fair trade.

8. Ibid.

4

International Trade, Technology Transfer, National Security, and Diplomacy

CONTROLLING TECHNOLOGY TRANSFER

Trade, technology transfer as part of trade, and national security interact in complex ways that affect the U.S. economy and the U.S. position in the international marketplace. The most visible traditional involvement of the U.S. government with the air transport and aircraft manufacturing industries has been through three categories of activities: (1) regulation of air transport, administration of air traffic control, certification of aircraft, and the funding of airways infrastructure--airports and air traffic control systems, and R&D related to the latter; (2) the funding of research and technology development through the National Aeronautics and Space Administration (NASA) and DOD; and (3) the funding of DOD-contracted development and engineering. Items (2) and (3), of course, have a major influence on the pace and direction of aeronautical technology development.

The government is also increasingly involved in technology transfer, not just through NASA and its unclassified civil R&D, but also through DOD military programs with our allies. Inevitably, such cooperative programs result in the transfer of military technologies, many of which are applicable to civil aircraft as well. The increasing proclivity to use control of international trade as an instrument of foreign policy adds further complexity to the issue.

Control of the export of technology--either in direct form or when embedded in advanced equipment--in the interests of national security is unquestionably a legitimate responsibility of government. The task requires balancing national security or foreign policy objectives with those of strengthening the economy and preserving the U.S. position in advanced technology. This balancing process inherently produces occasional inconsistencies and is vulnerable to indecision, which in itself is detrimental to trade. The U.S. aircraft manufacturing industry is inevitably a participant in this process. With exports now representing about two-thirds of sales of large jets and external markets projected to continue to grow more rapidly than domestic ones, the impact of export restrictions intended to limit and control technology transfer can become serious indeed.

One consequence is to cast a shadow over the reliability of U.S. manufacturers as sources of supply: the U.S. government may unilaterally terminate sales of aircraft, engines, and parts, and products manufactured by foreign companies may be cut off from U.S. components.

Questions that should be addressed in policy deliberations on the control of technology transfer include the following:

• How effective will given restraints be? And for how long?

• What alternatives are available to the foreign country or firm?

• What avenues for retaliation or compensatory action by foreign competitors or customers are available for both near and long term?

• What near-term and long-term commercial damage will U.S. firms suffer?

• What damage will the U.S. economy suffer?

With respect to the first and second questions, the growing technological parity shown by the competitive evaluation of technology by this panel leads increasingly to the answer that the foreign firm simply turns to another source of supply--even if it has to develop one (e.g., the certification of the Aeritalia G222 transport with Rolls Royce Tyne engines instead of CT64 engines so that the plane could be sold to Libya). With respect to the other questions, the evaluation should consider more than the possible loss of sales on a particular transaction. The result could be not only permanent loss of a particular market (because the customer resolves not to be trapped again), but also the creation of new competitors who could challenge in other markets as well (e.g., Airbus Industrie's plan to develop a European environmental control system for the A320 to replace the Garrett system used on the A300 and A310).

The panel is concerned about the effectiveness of the institutional mechanisms for addressing this complex policy issue. National security and foreign policy have powerful and articulate advocates within the institutional structure of government. Marshalling and integrating the interests of the private sector is complex, and the institutional mechanisms for doing so are comparatively much less well structured. Even within aircraft manufacturing, the interests and priorities of the large transport, commuter, business aircraft, and helicopter manufacturers are diverse, not to mention those of the thousands of component manufacturers.

This already complex problem is further complicated by the fact that the United States approaches this issue with a quite different perspective from that of its allies. The United States has tended to place highest priority on national and mutual security. Our allies, who expect us to take the lead in security, give greater weight to furthering economic growth. Furthermore, and especially in the area of foreign policy, the U.S. purview tends to be global, while that of NATO emphasizes Europe and nearby regions. In all cases it is important to recognize that technology has value only in a limited time frame. If the rules and procedures preclude its commercial application during this "window," its value deteriorates drastically.

Licensing and Coproduction

The United States has had a longstanding policy of cooperation through coproduction and licensing of American military aircraft and components with its industrialized allies (mainly NATO and Japan). The objective of this policy has been to enable allied nations to contribute to their mutual security with their own funds and industrial resources, by manufacturing and developing standard materiel of U.S. design. This program also reduces the drain on their foreign currency and engenders a greater feeling of partnership in mutual defense.

The details of this policy have changed substantially during the last 25 years. From 1955 to 1970 the primary mechanism for industrial cooperation in weapon systems was that of grant aid and foreign production of U.S. systems by allied nations under license. Examples of such "coproduction" agreements with NATO allies include production of the F-104 in Canada, Germany, Holland, Italy, and Japan, and production of various military rotorcraft in Britain and Italy.[1]

These coproduction agreements began with repair and maintenance and U.S. export of "knockdown" kits for assembly in the licensee nation. This was followed by a gradual increase in content manufactured in the licensee nation. The agreements served as important conduits for the transfer of manufacturing technology, as well as more limited transfer of design skills and data.

The magnitude of the transfer of technology through these coproduction agreements is very difficult to document. However, such licensed production undoubtedly helped create the manufacturing base for the European rotorcraft industry, and supported indirectly the growth of European components design and production capability. The Japanese aircraft industry was destroyed in World War II and stayed moribund until component repair work began for the U.S. Air Force during the Korean War. In 1960, for the same objective of national security, the U.S. government approved the F104J program for Japan. This program transferred modern production technology and created a production base in Japan.[2] However, it is doubtful whether such coproduction agreements directly or materially aided European prime contractor capabilities in large commercial transports, or current business or commuter aircraft design and development.

With the growth in size and sophistication of their defense industrial bases, the NATO countries began to seek a more substantial role as partners with the United States in the coproduction of complex systems and as suppliers of systems and components to the U.S. market. The arrangement for the coproduction of the F-16 was an early example of European (NATO) success in obtaining offsets in exchange for the purchase of U.S. aircraft.

The subject of mutual defense is beyond the scope of this study, but in the area of aircraft it is one in which the United States and its allies have somewhat opposing views. The United States wants its allies to bear their share of the cost of the joint aeronautical military establishment, and it exerts heavy pressure to adopt American equipment. Carried to extreme, that policy would leave Europeans totally dependent on U.S. aeronautical development and production capability--a position hardly consistent with mutuality. The European allies believe an indigenous aeronautical capability is not only vital to their internal security, but also to a viable mutual defense arrangement. The United States cannot be consistent in asserting the vital synergisms from a common civil-military aeronautical base for the United States without recognizing the applicability of this concept to Europe as well. Viewed from this vantage point, if it is in national security interests of the United States for Europe to have a viable military aircraft manufacturing establishment, we must recognize the legitimacy of Europe's interests in establishing a viable industry in civil aircraft manufacture.

President Carter endorsed the policy of the "two-way street" in NATO procurement in 1977. This was intended to result in increased U.S. purchases of European systems and components. The "two-way street" policy was initiated to prevent Europe from undertaking diverging military development, but the desire to achieve greater standardization and interoperability of NATO weapons was an additional reason that received publicity. It was apparent that continued U.S. access to the European military market was dependent on programs that enabled the Europeans to attain a less secondary role in aircraft manufacture. The French, meanwhile, continued to develop a competing capability. The sheer magnitude of the U.S. defense effort, and especially the huge R&D effort, has meant that the "street" was never "two-way."

This policy of reciprocal procurement has been carried out through the negotiation of bilateral Memoranda of Understanding (MOU) with the other NATO governments. Under the terms of the policy, the competitions of the U.S. and foreign signatory nations for military procurement are to be open to the foreign signators. As part of these MOUs exchanges of advanced technical data are mandated in order to provide a sound, even base for competition.

The legal status of the MOU is somewhat cloudy: it is a bilateral Executive agreement over which Congress has very limited powers of review or approval. Industry spokesmen have felt that MOUs are negotiated with insufficient input from American industry. DOD is perceived as seeking some sort of quid pro quo in negotiating an MOU, but the thing(s) sought do not necessarily have anything to do with technology or commerce. The panel believes that the defense establishment is perceived as being very aware of and concerned about the possible loss of critical technology through commercial channels, but much less sensitive to the possible adverse commercial implications of military agreements for coproduction. It is asserted that too many data and too much technology of a proprietary nature and having commercial applications are being transferred abroad with too little reciprocal flow. Design techniques and detailed data that are much more technologically advanced than was the case under early license coproduction agreements are now subject to transfer. Thus, the newer form of allied cooperation is considered to have a higher potential for adversely affecting the competitive status of the U.S. commercial aircraft industry than may have been realized and considered in the decision to support this DOD technology transfer process.

Frequently, the MOUs governing the "two-way street" via NATO procurements have obligated U.S. firms to make significant portions of their technology or research findings and know-how available to foreign firms. This transfer of technology involves "disembodied" product design data and production techniques. Consequently, this process represents a potentially more damaging channel of technology transfer than does direct coproduction itself.

The inadequacy of opportunity to provide input on MOU negotiations is of concern to representatives of industry. Care must be exercised if expanded congressional review is adopted as the solution. Recent congressional attempts to enforce "Buy American" policies (e.g., the strategic metals clause and the

Martin-Baker ejection seat episodes)[3] have placed U.S. producers in an indefensible position. Through MOUs, DOD development centers transfer advanced technology abroad, much of it applicable to both civil and military applications. At the same time, Congress presses for protectionist actions that raise the possibility of European retaliation against U.S. exports of aircraft components and systems.

The balance of defense trade is still in favor of the United States, in part due to two factors: the large U.S. investment in military R&D creates effective advanced technology systems, and the large U.S. purchases drive manufacturing costs down to levels others find difficult to match.

The panel believes that these arrangements have benefited the United States. They have undoubtedly played an important role in preserving the unity and commitment of our NATO allies. Furthermore, in the early stages--over two decades ago--they contributed to rebuilding the industrial base of Europe and Japan when cold war concerns were high. The important policy question is the need to reflect the changing environment for U.S. products: much greater economic strength among allies, much more comparable technological capability of international competitors, and increased importance of international markets for U.S. manufacturers.

Japanese-American Cooperation

Japanese-American cooperation in weapons production represents a special case. Due to self-imposed prohibitions on weapons exports, Japanese industry does not at present have the option of selling systems to the United States or others. Export to the United States of certain electronic components with military applications is already a highly sensitive political issue within Japan. Accordingly, coproduction has remained the primary channel for joint support of weapons procurement.

Recent cases of coproduction MOUs with Japan include the F-15 fighter and the associated F-100 engine. While these are highly sophisticated aircraft technologies, their direct, near-term spillover to commercial applications is relatively modest. However, this MOU followed a long list of similar agreements (e.g., P2V, T-33, F-104, F4, and P-3C aircraft as well as T58 and J79 engines) that in the aggregate significantly enhanced Japanese manufacturing capability. There has not been a large impact on the present ability of Japanese firms to operate as prime contractors for large transports or engines, or for regional aircraft.

Japan has been active on a modest scale in the area of turbine-powered business aircraft. Since their introduction in

1966, 749 Mitsubishi MU2 series turboprops have been sold. The Mitsubishi Diamond, a small turbojet, appeared in 1982. With the sale of nine aircraft, it obtained a 3 percent market penetration. It is likely, however, that the technology, materials, machine tools, and labor skills transferred through Japanese-American coproduction of military aircraft have strengthened the position of Japanese firms as subcontractors and/or vendors in future commercial jet transport projects. It appears that this is the policy being pursued by Japan. The real and projected impact of coproduction with Japan may be both to weaken the subcontractor infrastructure of the U.S. aircraft industry and to provide the base for future Japanese aircraft. It should be understood, however, that Japan has paid for this technology transfer through higher costs than would have been incurred in bringing aircraft from the United States. For example, the first lot of 90 F-15Js produced by Japan cost $45 million each. If purchased in the U.S. the aircraft would have been priced at $25 million each. Thus, it cost Japan $1.8 billion extra to produce the aircraft in Japan and to acquire associated skills. It is reasonable to assume that one objective in incurring the cost was to help develop an indigenous technology base.

Interaction with Foreign Policy

Exports of aircraft, as well as of other high-technology products, are controlled by the U.S. government, sometimes with the intent of influencing both the foreign and the domestic policies of other countries and of limiting the flow of advanced technology to Communist bloc countries. As a result, U.S. civil aircraft export controls are sometimes exercised in a manner that removes U.S. aircraft products from competition in some foreign markets. Other countries do the same, but the large U.S. share of aircraft exports makes U.S. activities more prominent.

This situation obviously favors foreign competitors whose governments view security and trade relationships differently. It has important long-term implications; consequences need to be weighed carefully. This situation can have the following impacts: it can contribute to the growth and power of competitors and even foster the creation of competitors whose governments do not agree with or wish to support U.S. policy, or view commerce as independent of foreign policy; it can contribute to the image of U.S. companies as unreliable sources of supply, not only for initial purchases but perhaps more importantly, for continuing product support (as in the case of French efforts to "de-Americanize" the Airbus); it can also permanently remove some markets from U.S. participation by allowing foreign competitors to develop "ground floor" positions from which they can be dislodged only with great difficulty. This latter situation applies to manufacturers of parts and components as well as complete aircraft.

The influence of U.S. control has been extended by getting other allied exporting nations to acknowledge U.S. sanctions with respect to reexport to third countries. This has placed the U.S. policy position on firmer international ground but given foreign exporters additional incentive to move toward the deletion of U.S.-supplied content in their aircraft products.

It is important to recognize the realities of the present competitive world with respect to export controls, commerce, and technology. Denial of access to technology that already exists elsewhere or that can easily be developed by competitors does little to preserve U.S. security and damages the U.S. competitive trade position. It forces the acceleration of the development of in-country technology, thereby creating new competition.

Achieving Balance in Controlling Technology Transfer

In assessing the desirability of controls on the export of U.S. technologies and proprietary data in aircraft, it is important to recognize that technological advancement in aviation has always involved two-way flows. A U.S. policy that leads to excessive restrictions on technology exchanges with other nations can threaten to impede reverse flow and thus impair the aeronautics infrastructure of this country. This reverse flow will become more important as other countries' R&D creates new technology, e.g., eutectic alloys in France and ceramics in Japan. There are major cultural, political, and economic offsets that must also be considered with respect to a fundamental change in the nation's historic open-door policies, which capitalized extensively on European aircraft technology before World War II.

It is equally important for the present status of U.S. technology vis-à-vis that available from others to be appraised realistically. For example, control of technology transfer for electronics and avionics has become very difficult. The commercialization of computer memories and data communication devices has diffused this technology all over the world. The United States does not hold technology leads in all areas, note, e.g., the powerful role of Japan in memories and data management.

This discussion is not intended to lead to the conclusion that the panel is opposed to U.S. government control of technology transfer. Rather, the panel recognizes the complexity of the issues.

In the light of these complexities the panel recommends that mechanisms be developed that will insure an effective industrial input to the deliberations on coproduction and technology transfer and that due weight be given to the change in competitive status and relative technological position in U.S. industry in reaching decisions.

If technology is to be controlled, it is important for the control to be effective, i.e., that there not be adequate alternatives available to the other side. It is also important to identify and give adequate weight to possible long-term adverse effects on the competitive position of U.S. industry. The cumulative effect of a deterioration in the competitive position of the U.S. aircraft industry has obvious strategic implications for the nation.

SYNERGY BETWEEN NATIONAL SECURITY AND CIVIL AVIATION

Leadership in aviation in support of the strategic strength of the United States has been a prime element of U.S. policy since World War II. In many respects leadership in the air has replaced the concept of power on the seas as a symbol of national strength.

The recent study by the Office of Science and Technology Policy (OSTP), noted in Chapter 1, in which both the National Security Council and DOD participated, reaffirmed the vital role of civil aviation--both aircraft manufacturers and air transport-- to the strategic posture of the United States.

The relationships between civil and military aviation are important to the health of each. A healthy civil industry is vital for national security and for wartime surge readiness, including the potential of elements of the civil transport system as a military reserve fleet in an emergency. Consequently, policy decisions that adversely affect the civil side of aviation can also impair the security of the nation.

Dual Use

The 15,000-company supplier base is an important key, since these firms supply critical materials and parts to both the civil and military aircraft industry. Frequently, in the case of smaller second- or third-tier suppliers, the military and civil production outputs are sufficiently common that the same facilities and labor pools produce both. U.S. requirements for military production have diminished substantially in recent years, representing about 37 percent of aircraft output compared with 53 percent in the period 1968 to 1972, during the Vietnam war. They are now increasing again as a result of increased DOD expenditures. Thus, civil aircraft production provides a vital stabilizing influence on the industry in the presence of continuing military procurement uncertainties.

Despite the differing requirements for civil and military aircraft, the technology base, much of the supplier base, and the skills and processes used are essentially common. They become mutually supportive in attaining diverse civil and military objectives. The technological synergies are very constructive. Military developments stress performance, while commercial aircraft developments emphasize lowered production costs, vehicle operating efficiency, and high availability with low maintenance--attributes that are valuable to the military establishment.

Historically, civil aeronautics development was triggered by military advancements, which the civil industry could refine or improve to gain the efficiency or technical objectives required in civil application--for example, the swept-wing, fly-by-wire controls, and retractable landing gear. In more recent years, a reverse situation has become common, with the results of civil research or component design subsequently being used for military purposes, e.g., improved fuel efficiency, maintainability and reliability of jet engines, super-aluminum alloys, flight management systems, and composite structures.

DOD has sponsored basic advances in propulsion technology in areas such as high-temperature materials, high pressure ratio compressors, combustion, etc. Although technology on supersonic engines and their integration into the inlet and exhaust systems of supersonic aircraft has little commercial relevance, other military engines for bombers, transports, patrol aircraft, and helicopters share common performance requirements with commercial aircraft. Both seek low fuel consumption, high thrust-weight ratio, long life, and high reliability. The need for high pressure ratio-high temperature engines is also common to both.

Technology developed for commercial requirements also benefits military applications. Commercial engines gain service experience 10 to 15 times faster than military engines, even military transport engines. To stay competitive, commercial engines are under continuing pressure to improve fuel efficiency, reliability, and service life--all resulting in significant cost savings to the user. The benefits of these advances, with their large base of in-service verification, recycle back into military engines. For example, some of the improvements in the CF6 turbofan engine (derived from the TF39 used in DOD's large C5A cargo airplane), developed during commercial service, are being incorporated in later versions of the TF39. Thus, commercial experience provides the DOD with better engines for transport and mission support aircraft than would have been produced by military experience alone.

The traditional role of DOD in propulsion development is changing. DOD is now supporting the launch of far fewer aircraft than was the case in previous decades. Equally important, for the last 15 years DOD has tended to define its interests more narrowly, to fund less generic research, and to insist on a specific, demonstrable relevance to present or proposed weapons systems for all DOD-sponsored R&D. For all but advanced supersonic aircraft or highly specialized mission requirements, DOD is largely prepared to buy off-the-shelf engine technology. Because of the huge investment ($1.5 to $2 billion) required and the long interval involved in the development of a new engine (four to six years), the future of U.S. technological leadership in propulsion will continue to rest to a large degree on defense sponsorship. Thus, an issue is evolving as to whether or how U.S. leadership in propulsion technology can be sustained in the face of this changing posture for DOD.

There are, however, some military requirements that do not place important demands for specialized performance on suppliers. These aircraft, which provide support services, include general personnel and supply transport, navigation and command control trainers, and in-flight refuelers. The C140A (Jetstar), U-8F (Seminole), T-39A (Saberliner), E-3 (707), E-4 (747), C-9A (DC-9), and KC-10 (DC-10) are examples of civil aircraft that have evolved into dual-use aircraft with major cost avoidance to the nation. Recent examples are the Learjet 35A--designated C-21A, and Beech Super King Air--designated B 200C for support functions.*

Our allies and international competitors provide explicitly for military support of commercial aircraft development. For example, the new British Aerospace AR146 commuter is being purchased by the Royal Air Force, and a version of the Bandeirante commuter is being purchased by the Brazilian Air Force. Obviously, it would be inappropriate for DOD to purchase civilian aircraft just to support the industry. However, at present no effective mechanisms exist even for joint consideration of military needs and civilian applications in planning development of civilian aircraft and in timing procurement. Generally, the military establishment has filled its support-aircraft requirements through existing civil production aircraft or called for new specialized developments when it saw a need. Planning military requirements for these support aircraft with a view to their integration with civilian developments could help U.S. manufacturers become more competitive by spreading the cost of design, development, and procurement among both military and civil users.

It is important to note, however, that the common use of aircraft or even joint development of support aircraft, while enhancing new starts and potentially reducing costs of systems, has at best a modest impact on the technological competitiveness of U.S. aircraft in the international arena. It could perhaps have greatest impact on regional transports and business aircraft.

What is more critical is that there be an effective national coupling between all areas of research and development that are pertinent to both military and civil systems. This would include appropriate areas of DOD-sponsored research and development, the generic work conducted under NASA sponsorship, and that which is privately funded. The FAA, which also contributes to this technology through its support of aircraft safety, flight operation, and related certification research technology and development, should be included in the coupling. This R&D is the foundation for the advanced U.S. position in power plants, controls, aerodynamics, structures, and aircraft operations for both military and commercial applications.

The panel recommends that the DOD, NASA, and the FAA reexamine the mechanisms for working with the civil aircraft manufacturers to insure that maximum advantage is taken of opportunities for dual-use capabilities in technology development for design, manufacture, and certification.

Timing of Procurement

Ensuring reasonably level support for the production base through timing of purchases would help both military and civil activity. This help would be most meaningful in the areas of regional transports, business aircraft, and rotorcraft. Procurement of military aircraft is characterized by wild fluctuations, and such variations play havoc with utilization of facilities and retention of key human resources. For example, virtually no military helicopters were purchased during the 1970s. Manufacture of civilian helicopters preserved the industry. Recent military orders are now capitalizing on the infrastructure so preserved.

Large civil transports represent a special situation. DOD has identified a strategic gap in the adequacy of reserve air transport to meet emergencies. The civil transport fleet can provide some support in a reserve role, but the fact that the aircraft were not designed for that purpose limits their usefulness. One option is for DOD to subsidize the extra expense that would be incurred in developing a special fleet of civilian aircraft to serve explicitly as a reserve. When budget priorities are being established, DOD has not seen fit to allocate resources to such a task, and the panel is not in a position to recommend changes in DOD priorities. With regard to large civil transports, DOD has examined the issue of reserve transport needs and the role of the civil transport fleet. These issues are not fully resolved. Obviously, the resolution of the reserve fleet issue can affect large aircraft procurement considerations and is of special interest to the manufacturing and air transportation industries.

The panel recognizes the difficulties of achieving more stable procurement of military aircraft. Nevertheless, the production base plays a vital role in surge capacity. Stability of operations contributes to maintaining the readiness of that production base and indirectly strengthening the competitive capability of civil activity. Consequently, renewed efforts are needed to reduce the wide swings in military procurement (in the absence of any emergency) that affect the base so adversely.

The panel recommends that DOD and industry seek to strengthen coordinated planning for aircraft procurement to reduce as far as practicable the great cyclicality in production that disrupts the industry.

NOTES

1. Alan I. Rapoport, and Carol Erlebach, Collaborative Projects Between the United States and Foreign Aeronautics Industries, Division of Policy Research and Analyses, National Science Foundation, October 1982.

2. (a) G.R. Hall, and R.E. Johnson, "Transfers of United States Aerospace Technology to Japan," The Technology Factor in International Trade, a Conference of the Universities-National Bureau Committee for Economic Research, National Bureau of Economic Research, Columbia University Press, New York, 1970.

(b) U.S. General Accounting Office, U.S. Military Coproduction Programs Assist Japan in Developing Its Civil Aircraft Industry, A report by the Comptroller General to the Subcommittee on Ways and Means, U.S. House of Representatives, March 18, 1982.

(c) U.S. House of Representatives, Trade with Japan, hearings before the Subcommittee on Trade of the Committee on Ways and Means, U.S. House of Representatives, 96th Congress, Second Session, Washington, D.C., 1980.

(d) United States Trade Council, Japan's Aircraft Industry, Washington, D.C., January 11, 1980.

3. Great Britain secured a position on a U.S. fighter with the Martin-Baker ejection seat in an open competition. Subsequently, as a result of pressure from U.S. industry, Congress mandated use of a U.S. product instead. The action caused great resentment in Great Britain.

4. Aviation Week and Space Technology, September 26, 1983, p. 26.

5
Competitive Assessment of Technology

In reviewing the history of the United States in world commercial aviation, it is obvious that the ability to translate high technology into efficient products suited to the marketplace has been a major factor in penetrating world markets successfully. Of comparable importance, manufacturers and customer airlines have been willing to incorporate even newer technologies as they emerged, both for new aircraft and for modification of existing models to improve their performance. The U.S. response to the need for quiet engines, reduction in fuel consumption, and the incorporation of new materials is an example of its continuing ability and readiness to utilize new technology. The airlines of the United States, other national markets, and the certifying agencies have fulfilled an essential role in supporting acceptance of these technologies and in demonstrating them through safe and cost-effective service. None of this would have been possible without the active participation, encouragement, and support of the U.S. Federal Aviation Administration (FAA) in achieving early certification.

Technological leadership in the commercial aircraft field is not of itself sufficient for success in the marketplace. The products must fit the customer's needs and be available when the customer wants them. When the United States dominated the large transport and other aircraft markets, the time of introduction and the fit of the product to a specific customer's needs were important but not as overriding as today. Two things have happened to suggest that the United States must accelerate its application of technology: Effective foreign competition has emerged with equivalent technology and a number of additional countries such as Indonesia, Brazil, Spain, and Japan have indicated their determination to enter some segments of the market.

This chapter consists of two parts. The first addresses the airframe and the fully assembled aircraft; the second examines propulsion technology. In each the panel assesses the present state of technology, then considers capabilities for conducting research and development and for manufacture.

105

AIRFRAME AND FULLY ASSEMBLED AIRCRAFT

The following technologies associated with the airframe and fully assembled aircraft have been identified as fundamental to the future competitive posture of U.S. civil aviation:

1. Design techniques
   Advanced computational analysis
   Design optimization and integration (computer-aided design/computer-aided manufacture--CAD/CAM)
2. Aerodynamics
   Active boundary layer management (including laminar flow control)
3. Flight controls
   Relaxed stability (reduced tail and wing size)
   Active controls (wingload alleviation and flutter suppression)
4. Advanced structures
   Advanced metallic alloys (including superplastic forming)
   Metal bonding techniques
   Composite structures
5. Propulsion integration
   Integrated engine/nacelle/airframe
   Advanced propellers and gearboxes
6. Avionics
   Ultrareliable, fault-tolerant systems
   Advanced flight decks ("all glass cockpit")
   Computer-integrated flight management

The combination of the key technologies listed above, when fully integrated into an all-new aircraft design, could improve its fuel efficiency by as much as 30 to 50 percent--and some industry experts are even more optimistic. During the past 20 years, the propulsion system provided the most significant gains. In the next 20 years, the propulsion system will again provide improvements, but they will be accompanied by improvements in aerodynamics, structures, avionics, controls, and systems. Figure 5-1, adapted from a paper by NASA, illustrates how these technology improvements can be combined over the remainder of this century to produce these large benefits. The propulsion system gain does not include the effects of advanced turboprops or propfans, which could provide an additional 20 percent improvement. If the recently conceived unducted fan concept is successful propfans would achieve improvements in efficiency of 30 to 35 percent. The viability of future new civil aircraft will depend on the ability to develop and implement these technologies in a cost-effective and timely manner.

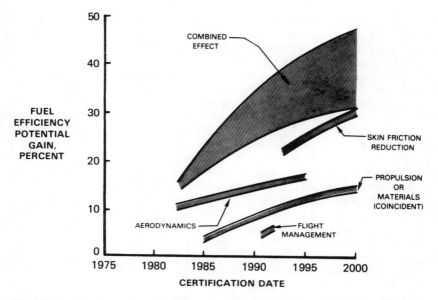

FIGURE 5-1 Benefits Possible From Technology Improvements

SOURCE: Derived from NASA Technology Program for Future Civil Air Transports; H.T. Wright, Aerospace Industries Association of America, International Air Transportation Conference, June 1983, Montreal, Canada.

Status of Technology Design Techniques

The capabilities of modern high-speed computers have made possible the use of very sophisticated techniques for computational analysis in both aerodynamics and structures. Recent advances in computational aerodynamics have allowed transonic drag rise characteristics to be determined with a high degree of accuracy, thus allowing designers to develop airfoil shapes quickly to meet a variety of requirements. Computational aerodynamics techniques are also being applied to nacelle cowl design, after-body design, and nacelle placement relative to the wing. The effect of these techniques is to reduce dependence on empiricism and experiment and to use fewer, but more representative wind tunnel tests for validation. The technology is also applicable to design processes for rotorcraft and general aviation craft.

United States manufacturers are making extensive use of these techniques in design studies of the next-generation 150-seat aircraft. Airbus Industrie is exploiting ongoing European research programs in computer-aided airflow modeling of the A320 wing. The goal is further reduction of drag while maximizing aerodynamic and structural efficiency.

In structural analysis, the United States retains a lead in the ability to optimize designs through use of modern mathematical models in conjunction with modern large-capacity computers. In basic advanced wing design the status of the United States appears to be comparable with others. However, in transonic wing design, the United States is believed by the panel to have a slight lead over Europe and probably a larger lead over Japan due to pioneering supercritical wing work by NASA, which has been extended by U.S. airframe manufacturers and NASA.

Computer-aided design and computer-aided manufacturing (CAD/CAM) are key new design techniques brought about by the revolution in interactive software developed for modern high-speed computers. CAD systems provide the capability for analyzing many different designs quickly and accurately. System optimization of complex interactive elements can now be easily accomplished, thus minimizing design lead time and cost. CAM systems allow selected designs to flow directly to the manufacturing process by providing computer-developed instructions for numerically controlled machines. About one-third of the Boeing 767 components were designed with the help of a computer, and about 5 percent of the B-767 design went straight from computer-aided design into numerically controlled machining. The resulting reduction in drawing errors is a major benefit as work is released onto the production line.

Pioneered in this country, CAD/CAM technology has been quickly adopted abroad and is now standard practice at Airbus Industrie and in Japan. With the Messerschmitt (MBB) computer-aided design techniques, which are widely used for lofting and autodrafting, peaks and troughs of new design tasks can be handled without attendant manpower fluctuations. Ease of access by foreigners to CAD/CAM hardware and software developed in the United States assures that the European and Japanese aerospace industries can stay competitive in this technology in the future.

The panel believes that not enough attention is being paid to the application of those powerful CAD/CAM tools to smaller aircraft. Thus, the U.S.-manufactured aircraft for small feeder lines and for limited markets, such as executive aircraft, may not be realizing their full technological potential and obtaining as strong a market position as possible.

Aerodynamics

In addition to the advances in aerodynamic computational procedures, significant potential exists for advances in aerodynamics in the areas of boundary layer management for cruise conditions and lift enhancement for takeoff and landing. Figure 5-1 indicates the gains to be realized from the successful attainment of laminar flow to reduce skin friction drag. In the past three decades extensive analytical and experimental work has been done in this country under NASA sponsorship to understand the laminar- to turbulent-flow transition and to develop methods for delaying this transition. Much more work needs to be done to adapt these methods to a large commercial transport in a practical, cost-effective manner. Current NASA plans call for testing the most promising configurations in actual flight conditions. Should these tests prove successful, adaptation of this technology to a new production aircraft is not expected before the mid- to late 1990s, 10 to 15 or more years from now.

The status of active boundary layer management programs in Europe is unknown at this time, but the United States is thought to be ahead, based on the extensive NASA work discussed above.

The Japanese are developing an experimental "Quiet STOL" research aircraft using the upper-surface blowing concept similar to NASA's QSRA aircraft and Boeing's YC-14 STOL Transport Demonstrator Aircraft for DOD.

In the low-speed, high-lift flight regime, current transports incorporate a combination of leading edge devices and sophisticated flaps to vary wing camber to increase lift at low speeds. Significant advances in multielement airfoil analysis techniques are providing considerable insight into the behavior of high-lift systems and reducing the need for extensive experimental data.

The United States and Europe are thought to be generally comparable in wing design, e.g., the Airbus A310 wing incorporates the latest in high-lift systems to provide excellent takeoff and landing performance. Extensive double curvature in the lower skin of the inner wing provides optimum lift characteristics. Precise altitude control, combined with thrust control through flight path computers, provides the capability for Category III automatic landing in which conditions are virtually zero ceiling, zero visibility.

Improvements in aerodynamics are not receiving particular attention in aircraft for general aviation, but the strength of the United States in this field could accrue to U.S. manufacturers if it is applied. In rotorcraft, foreign capability is judged to be on a par with the United States--though foreign manufacturers have been able to supply advanced technologies more rapidly.

Flight Controls

Active control systems that could allow reduced static longitudinal stability are conceptually possible for transport aircraft, with resulting reductions in drag and weight due to reduced tail and wing areas. However, further research and development effort is required for large-scale applications. The next generation of 150-seat transports is expected to use augmented stability systems to provide a tail designed to accommodate a center of gravity located aft, thus minimizing trim drag. U.S. manufacturers and Airbus appear to be approximately equal in this technology. Full exploitation of this technology will require another round of aircraft development.

The use of limited active controls for wind-gust and maneuver-load alleviation has already been incorporated in the Lockheed L-1011-500. This technology can allow reductions in wing structural weight or further increases in wing aspect ratio to improve performance without weight increase. Flutter suppression modes offer further improvements for more advanced aircraft. Application of this technology is already being considered by Airbus for stretched versions of the A300 as well as for later versions of the A320, which is to have what is called a fly-by-wire control system. The Concorde was the first certificated commercial aircraft to rely principally on a fly-by-wire control system. It also contains a highly integrated stability augmentation control system. In this area of technology, the United States and Europe can be judged to be about equal in current capability.

General aviation airplanes tend to follow large aircraft in adopting advanced flight controls. In rotorcraft, the United States is thought to have the lead in flight control technology.

Advanced Structures

Recently, new high strength-to-weight aluminum-lithium alloys have shown potential for additional significant weight savings, but much work remains to be done in qualifying the material and scaling up its production in sheet, plate, and extruded forms before widespread application in aircraft manufacture can take place. Another emerging structural concept that shows much promise is superplastically formed, diffusion-bonded metals (notably titanium but also possibly aluminum).

Improved aluminum alloys are now being incorporated by Airbus in the A310. However, the "economic repair life" of the A310 is estimated by Airbus to be 40,000 cycles compared to Boeing's estimated life of 60,000 cycles for the 767. Comparisons of life, however, are dependent on the stress level chosen by the

designer for the structure in question. Newly developed
aluminum-zinc alloys with thermomechnical treatment for
increased compression strength and better fracture properties are
planned for the A320. More extensive use of titanium is also
planned for highly stressed parts. In these respects, Airbus
metallic structure technology is fully competitive with current
U.S. technology. Its research on advanced alloys of the
aluminum-lithium type and superplastic-formed, diffusion-bonded
titanium is approximately the same as in the United States.

To date, current and planned aircraft are minimizing use of
adhesive bonding due to poor early experience. Metal-to-metal
bonding technology applications in Europe are at least equivalent
to those in the U.S. where application to fuselage structure,
including compound-curved panels, is fully accepted, certified,
and demonstrated in extended operation of wide-bodied transports.

The largest single opportunity in airframe materials lies in
composite materials, including metal matrix composites. The
combination of thermoplastic or thermoset composites with the
attendant means of processing and fabricating technology is a
rapidly expanding field with very large potential payoff. Both
United States and European developers are active. European
research capabilities are almost equal to those in the U.S. During
the past few years, great strides have been made in the use of
advanced nonmetallic composite structural elements. These
composite structures have high stiffness and extremely light
weight when compared with conventional metal structures and
offer the promise of significant increases in performance, due to
the reduction in weight and the promise of extended life in overall
aircraft performance and efficiency.

The latest U.S. aircraft, such as the Boeing 767, incorporate
significant amounts of composites in secondary structures. More
advanced designs, such as the proposed McDonnell Douglas D-330
series, extend composites to more wing components, cabin floor
beams, the entire nacelle, and the tail cone (Figure 5-2).

European research and development efforts on composite
materials are extensive and continue to accelerate. Many European aerospace companies have been working with composite
materials for up to 15 years. These companies believe they have a
basic scientific understanding of the materials, which they are
now converting into practice. Airbus Industrie has a program for
the progressive introduction of composite components on the
A300 and the A310 (Figure 5-3). The A320 will add composite
elevators, fin and tail-plane trailing edges, floor panels, cowl
components, wing-to-body fairings, and carbon-composite wheel
brakes (Figure 5-4).

At present, relatively small elements such as rudders, ailerons,
and spoilers have been produced. In the long term, the full poten-

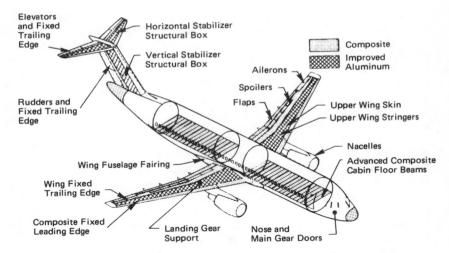

FIGURE 5-2 McDonnell Douglas D-3300 Advanced Material Applications

SOURCE: McDonnell Douglas.

tial of composite materials will be realized with their incorporation into primary aircraft structures such as wings, stabilizers, and fuselages. Benefits would potentially include a 15 to 25 percent reduction in structural weight, a 7 to 15 percent improvement in fuel efficiency, and resulting 4 to 8 percent reductions in direct operating cost. Projections of the latter are more uncertain because the manufacturing costs for composites and future costs for fuel are very uncertain.

In the United States a composite primary structure program was initiated by NASA in 1976, with the objective of developing the technology and confidence to permit commercial transport manufacturers to use composites extensively in the primary structure of production aircraft. The original plan to build and flight test a full-scale wing was regarded as too expensive. The program has been scaled back to build and test key components. Further specialized tests and the establishment of a resulting data base are still necessary to develop confidence in the application of composites to primary structures. NASA plans still call for fuselage design studies to begin this year, followed by a six-year fuselage test program. Similar plans, directed at demonstration of such structures for airline evaluation and assurance that certification is valid, have consistently been terminated during budget negotiations with OMB.

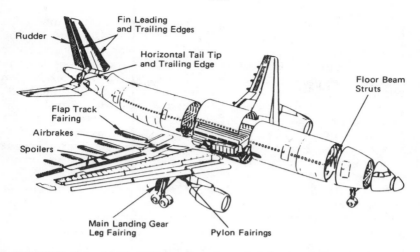

FIGURE 5-3 A300-600 Application of Advanced Composites

SOURCE: Airbus Brochure.

Airbus Industrie partners already have wide design/development/service experience including current service trials on A300s in airline use.

Initial Applications

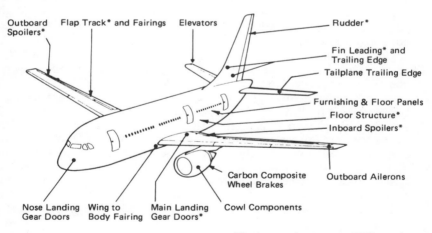

*Reads across from current A300 experience.

FIGURE 5-4 A320 Advanced Composite Materials

SOURCE: Airbus Brochure.

European industry use of primary composite structures has begun in military applications. Composites are also used for the pod for the Rolls Royce RB211 engine and for helicopter rotor blades and rotor heads. Composite research and development in Europe is now concentrated on ways to speed the production process and reduce costs through automation and other methods, as well as on postproduction testing and quality control. This indicates that Airbus will continue to be very aggressive in the application of composites to future aircraft, and given the moderate pace of the current NASA program and the budget pressures it is encountering, Airbus may take the lead in this very important technology.

In application of advanced structures to general aviation and regional aircraft, the United States is judged to have an advantage; however, in rotorcraft our position is regarded as no more than equal to that of foreign competitors--especially France.

Propulsion Integration

Propulsion integration of powerplant with wing or fuselage is a relatively mature art for conventional turbofan-powered aircraft. The United States and Europe are regarded as comparable. Analytical techniques are helping to optimize the location of engine nacelles relative to the wing for wing-mounted turbofan installations. Both U.S.- and British-designed nacelles have been applied to U.S. aircraft. The British nacelles show a slight advantage due primarily to shorter engine length. However, competitive nacelle technology is judged about equal.

Integration of the propulsion system with the airframe becomes extremely important when high-speed turboprop powerplants or propfans are used. This advanced technology is widely regarded, both in the U.S. and elsewhere, as holding great promise for improved fuel efficiency. It is especially applicable to general aviation aircraft and regional aircraft. As advanced turboprops exceed M = 0.70 (the region now being contemplated) interference drag becomes exceedingly critical, as do inlet recovery, flow distortion, and interference problems. Mathematical analyses of these complex three-dimensional flow fields are under way, but extensive wind tunnel and flight testing are required to verify and calibrate these analytical models before design decisions can be made.

Advanced turboprops also have to contend with high-decibel, and poorly understood, acoustic problems. Analytical models of propeller noise require full-scale flight test data for confirmation. Once propeller acoustic characteristics are understood, methods of minimizing noise and vibration in the passenger cabin must be developed and substantiated.

The development of advanced propellers and their gearboxes, or systems that eliminate the need for gearboxes, is central to incorporation of propfans and advanced transports. Aerodynamic performance of propfans has already been substantiated by tests. Structural design of the thin, swept blades and contrarotating configuration necessary for the higher Mach-number operation has not yet been proven at full scale. Extensive research and development work needs to be done on all aspects of advanced propeller systems before design of advanced high-speed turboprop transports can proceed confidently. Current U.S. propfan R&D is largely limited to NASA-sponsored programs, which are not scheduled to complete demonstration of systems integration in aircraft flight tests until 1988, providing funds are allocated. That schedule will not permit U.S. propfan development to start until the early 1990s at best. The U.S. propfan program has concentrated on very high speed props (M = 0.8), and in that speed range the United States is probably ahead in technology. However, economic studies suggest this speed may be too high. At slower speeds (M = 0.7), the cost per seat-mile is substantially lower, and the Europeans may not be behind, having considerable experience at M = 0.5.

The Airbus view of propfan technology would seem to indicate that it is wrestling with the same problems, and Airbus does not forecast an advanced propfan aircraft before the 1990s, if then. The French government has been sponsoring research into propfans for the last three years. How extensive this work is or what results have been achieved to date is not yet known.

In rotorcraft the United States is regarded as an equal in propulsion integration. The United States has a substantial technological lead in an advanced version of rotorcraft, the tilt rotor. NASA and the Army have recently validated a new concept in rotorcraft technology having potentially significant civil applications. The XV-15 tilt-rotor, proof-of-concept vehicle has demonstrated that the characteristics and capabilities of turboprop airplanes can be blended with those of helicopters in a single aircraft. DOD has moved rapidly to capitalize on this configuration via the Joint Services Vertical Lift Aircraft Program (JVX), now in preliminary design.

A civil derivative of the military JVX could yield a 30- to 40-passenger vertical-takeoff and -landing (VTOL) regional transport rotorcraft in the 35,000- to 45,000-pound gross weight class. The vehicle would be capable of cruising at speeds above 300 knots at altitudes of 25,000 to 30,000 feet over a range of 500 nautical miles. The aircraft would be a synthesis of advanced rotorcraft technology and the other technologies that have been noted.

Civil versions of the rotor could broaden the services provided by small regional aircraft and helicopters and increase the passenger capacity of limited airports.

Avionics

The application of digital electronics has already made major improvements in avionics systems capability and reliability while reducing weight, volume, and cost per unit of capability. The new generation of B-757, B-767, B737-300, MD-80, and A310 aircraft all utilize digital flight control systems. Major increases in the use of the latest developments in microcircuitry will permit the attainment of ultrareliable, fault-tolerant systems architecture. Such systems are vital to the implementation of active controls and computer-integrated flight management systems.

The forward-facing crew cockpit (FFCC) on the A310 is an advanced design comparable with the latest U.S. planes. However, it should be noted that the color CRT hardware essential to such systems was developed in Japan. Both Aerospatiale and British Aerospace are conducting advanced flight deck programs that have developed the use of multifunction CRT displays. Similar advanced crew stations are being developed by U.S. manufacturers. Advanced avionics, in conjunction with active controls and the incorporation of flight management systems, can potentially produce fuel savings of up to 20 percent, weight reductions of as much as 10 percent, with attendant reductions in operating cost of 5 to 10 percent.

The advances in avionics also have extensive room for application to general aviation and regional aircraft, and U.S. strength in this area is applicable to these classes of aircraft. In rotorcraft the U.S. is judged to have an advantage in both flight management and automated control.

Much of the electronics/avionics capability in commercial transports is the by-product of technology developed for military aircraft. This is as true for foreign countries as it is for the United States. In military avionics, the United States still leads the rest of the world; as long as the United States continues the close synergy between civil and military avionics technology, it is doubtful that any foreign country will soon surpass the United States in this technology.

However, as noted earlier, the Japanese did develop present aircraft-quality color CRT hardware for the European and U.S. aircraft industry. Japan does have the development capability and potentially lower costs that would enable it to challenge the U.S. leadership in aircraft avionics (digital computers), given the opportunity. Presently, flight deck and flight controls technology account for over 12 percent of the total aircraft price. Thus, with less expensive avionics in foreign aircraft, the U.S. competitive position could be jeopardized.

In summary, significant opportunities exist for further advances in technology. These advances will have their impact primarily in the production of aircraft that are lighter, more efficient, quieter, and more economical to operate. Thus, while they will lead to significant improvements in the economics of air transport, they are unlikely to affect the amenities that are more visible to the passenger--speed, comfort, and roominess.

The United States enjoys leadership or parity in all the important technologies, but in all cases the lead is small and our competitors have the necessary skills and knowledge to achieve leadership if our momentum falters. The area of greatest concern within the industry is its potential inability to translate advances in technology into new aircraft that incorporate the latest technology. The possibility of partnership between European and Japanese companies would lead to truly formidable competition.

Status of Research, Development, and Production Capabilities

Research Capabilities

Technology development starts at the level of the research laboratory. In the United States the prime aeronautical research facilities are those of the National Aeronautics and Space Administration (NASA), the U.S. Military Services, and the major airframe companies.

The capital investment in NASA test facilities and wind tunnels over the years has resulted in an extensive capability to support the requirements of research, design, and total systems tests for all aeronautical systems. The current replacement value of these federal facilities is estimated at approximately 10 billion dollars. Total NASA employment is currently 21,200 people, of whom 3,740 specialize in aeronautics.

Information on European research and technology efforts indicates strong concentration on many of the same concepts being pursued in the United States. Western European countries have some excellent aeronautical laboratory facilities and many excellent technical universities.

The National Research Facilities (similar to NASA) which support the major Airbus Industrie partner companies are:

Great Britain
Royal Aircraft Establishment (RAE)
Eight wind tunnels--7,300 people (1980)

France
    National Office for Aerospace Research (O.N.E.R.A.)
    Eight wind tunnels--1,900 people (1980)
Germany
    German Gas Dynamics Institute
    Seven wind tunnels--3,100 people (1980)

Total population of these three research facilities is 12,300, which is over half that of NASA's total of 21,200. The number of individuals in equivalent aeronautics work compared with NASA's 3,240 is not known, but is thought to be larger because of NASA's heavy emphasis on space technology. The United States high-speed tunnels are superior to those in Europe; however, low-speed and transonic tunnels are judged to be about equal in capability. All of these facilities should be on a par in 10 to 15 years.

The aeronautical technology in Japan lags far behind that of the United States. Japan's National Aerospace Laboratory (NAL) supports national R&D, but it has few adequate facilities for aeronautical research. While Japan's aircraft manufacturing industry is also comparatively small by Western standards, national plans call for expansion by redeployments from "maturing" industries, such as consumer electronics, shipbuilding, and autos.

Japanese civil R&D is further viewed as handicapped because there are no domestic commercial avionics outlets and little military spinoff. However, national policies endorse direct government support for basic and high-risk experimental and generic research. Aspects of Japanese research are of interest in a dual-use sense, and the Japanese recently agreed to specific technology exports of this nature that would benefit the military establishment in the United States. Japanese technical development programs are coordinated by the Ministry of International Trade and Industry (MITI).

Employment

In terms of major aerospace companies, the total employment of Airbus partner companies is roughly equivalent to that of Boeing and McDonnell Douglas combined (Figure 5-5). The United States figure is conservative because the Boeing and McDonnell Douglas numbers do not include the employees of the manufacturers of some major components built by others, whereas the Airbus numbers do. These figures include civil, military, and space-program personnel. Japan's big three companies--IHI, Mitsubishi, and Kawasaki--have an aerospace population of about 14,000, or slightly above half the Japanese total aerospace employment.

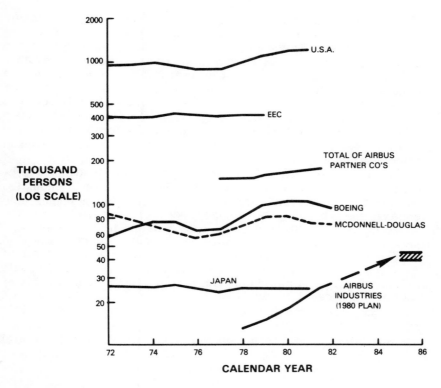

FIGURE 5-5 Aerospace Employment

SOURCE: Aerospace Facts and Figures, 1982/83; E.E.C. Staff Working Paper, Sec. (80)1287; Flight International, p. 1876, November 15, 1980; Annual Reports of Boeing and McDonnell Douglas; Airbus Industries Press Letter, August 1980.

According to an Airbus Industrie plan published in 1980, the number of Airbus partner company personnel engaged in the various Airbus programs is expected to grow to 40,000 or 45,000 by the mid-1980s (Figure 5-5). However, the worldwide recession of the last few years, which severely curtailed aircraft orders, has already significantly slowed implementation of this plan.

Facilities

A gross measure of the size of Airbus Industrie's facilities is the combined factory floor area of all the participating partners of Airbus Industrie, which is roughly comparable to that of Boeing and McDonnell Douglas combined. In both cases, these facilities are used for civil, military, and space systems; however, in the U.S. case, major aircraft components are subcontracted to other U.S. aerospace manufacturers, whereas the Airbus partnership manufactures all major components internally. If the total floor space of U.S. facilities devoted to the manufacture of Boeing and McDonnell Douglas products were combined, it would far exceed that of Airbus Industrie. As noted earlier, the production of the A320 is specifically intended to further strengthen European manufacturing capability.

A more meaningful comparison with Airbus Industrie's production capacity can be obtained from Figure 5-6, which indicates the monthly production rate of A300 aircraft (on a comparable empty-weight basis). The dashed line on Figure 5-6 shows the expected A300/A310 production rate buildup from the original 1980 plan. Delivery of the A320 is scheduled to commence in 1988. The slope since has changed, but the important point is that Airbus is putting in place facilities, tooling, and personnel capable of achieving a potential 10 per month production rate by the latter part of this decade.

British Aerospace (BAe) has tooled up to produce 98 A300/ A310 wing sets per year. Heretofore, British Aerospace was set up for low-volume production. It took a significant cultural

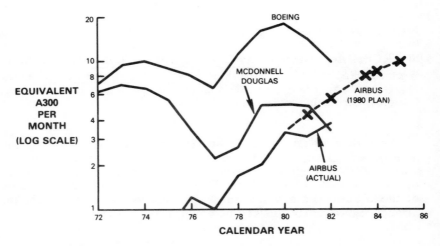

FIGURE 5-6 Comparative Aircraft Production Rates

SOURCE: Pratt and Whitney, based on data supplied by manufacturers.

change and major investment in new tools to reduce costs and increase production runs so that BAe could participate in the A300 program. BAe investment in new machining equipment and tooling for the Airbus Industrie program will total over $150 million by 1984.

Messerschmitt-Boekow-Blohm (MBB) of West Germany opened a new facility in 1979, which makes extensive use of numerically controlled machining. As a result, MBB productivity on A300/A310 parts has improved significantly. It appears to be on an 83 percent learning curve, which compares well with the best American practice. New investment in facilities and tooling is estimated by MBB to be $250 million (1979 dollars) with about a 30 percent increase in factory floor space.

Aerospatiale, in addition to building the cockpit, forward fuselage sections, and wing-carry-through structure of the A-300/A-310, has the responsibility for final assembly. Aerospatiale has recently invested some $200 million over a two-year period and will continue to invest at this rate. To the existing large final assembly plant at Toulouse is being added the equally large assembly hall formerly occupied by Concorde. An additional hall is also being built alongside, essentially tripling the existing A300 factory space. Aerospatiale has now moved to a two-shift operation, which required a significant change in the habits of the French work force. Third-shift operations are not envisioned.

The Japanese should not be underestimated. Although they lack the technology or capability to initiate a new large commercial aircraft program on their own, they would be formidable competitors as partners in an international joint venture. Major involvement in programs such as the F-15 and Boeing 767 transport is helping Japanese aeronautical production technology to become more competitive with the United States.

PROPULSION TECHNOLOGY

Status of Technology

The three free-world engine manufacturers currently producing large commercial transport turbofan engines are Pratt and Whitney, General Electric, and Rolls Royce. In addition to the three principal manufacturers, several European and Japanese manufacturers participate in licensing, coproduction, and codevelopment through agreements with the three principals. These participating companies are SNECMA (France), MTU (Germany), Volvo Flygmotor (Sweden), FIAT Aviazione (Italy), and Ishikawajima-Harima (IHI), Mitsubishi (MHI), and Kawasaki (KHI) in Japan.

This section assesses the U.S. manufacturers of large commercial transport engines compared with current and potential future foreign competitors. Areas of comparison discussed are: engine technologies and programs, development and production capabilities, and international joint ventures.

Among the most important technologies for turbojet and turbofan engines are the following: aerodynamics of rotating machinery (fans, compressors, and turbines); combustion; lightweight, high-strength and high-temperature materials; design and configuration; and engine controls. An overview assessment of U.S. and foreign technological strengths in these areas can be inferred by comparing the end results of the application of these technologies to resultant commercial turbofan engines.

Figures 5-7 through 5-9 chronologically compare three important overall parameters reflecting technology content in engines.

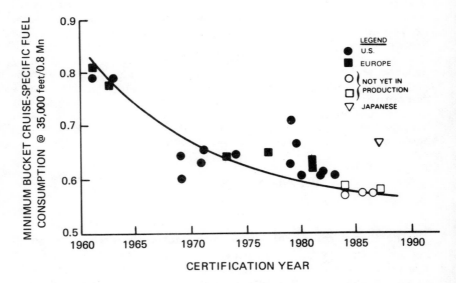

FIGURE 5-7 Commercial Transport Engines--Cruise Specific Fuel Consumption (manufacturer's quoted performance)

SOURCE: Pratt and Whitney, from data supplied by manufacturers.

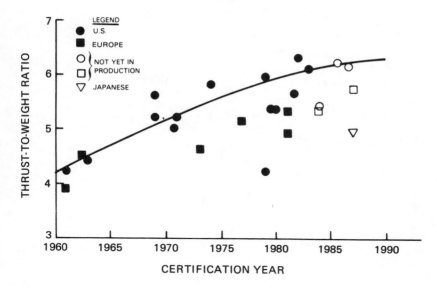

FIGURE 5-8 Commercial Transport Engines--Thrust-to-Weight Ratio (manufacturer's quoted performance)

SOURCE: Pratt and Whitney, from data supplied by manufacturers.

Decreasing Thrust Specific Fuel Consumption (TSFC) at Cruise (Figure 5-7) A measure of fuel efficiency of the engine. Advances in aerodynamics, high-temperature materials, and combustion technologies are important contributors to this parameter. Additionally, engine controls technology can contribute to overall aircraft-mission fuel efficiency by helping to minimize fuel consumption during taxiing, descent, and low-altitude holding. For example, on a flight from Chicago to Miami this noncruise fuel use can be as much as 11 percent of total trip fuel.

Increasing Engine Thrust-to-Weight Ratios (Figure 5-8) Technologies contributing significantly to this parameter are lightweight, high-strength, and high-temperature materials, as well as design and configuration.

Increasing Turbine Inlet Temperature (Figure 5-9). This parameter influences the fuel efficiency of the engine and is a con-

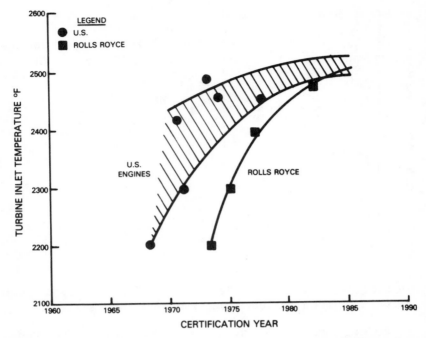

FIGURE 5-9 Commercial Transport Engines--Turbine Inlet Temperature (manufacturer's quoted performance)

SOURCE: Pratt and Whitney, from data supplied by manufacturers.

tributor to lighter weight. Improvements in combustion and high-temperature materials, along with turbine blade cooling design, are major contributors to this technology. Projections have been extended into the 1990s by including published engine data for future designs from the respective engine manufacturers.

Figures 5-7 through 5-9 include SNECMA's participation as a 50 percent codevelopment partner in the CFM56 and study engines such as the M56-2000, which it considered developing with 100 percent French financing and contracted technical assistance from General Electric. Also shown in the figures is the FJR710, an engine under development in Japan since 1971 and scheduled to power a four-engined, short-takeoff and -landing demonstrator aircraft in May 1984. The aircraft is being developed in Japan by the National Aerospace Laboratory. For the time period of its potential commercial availability, the FJR710 is not considered competitive in technology.

Rolls Royce Engine Technologies and Programs

Since the beginning of the jet-powered commercial transport era in the 1950s, Rolls Royce has been recognized by the U.S. engine manufacturers as serious competition. Until the advent of the wide-bodied commercial transports in the late 1960s, Rolls Royce engines mainly powered European-built aircraft such as the Comet, Caravelle, BAC-111, and Trident. In 1968, Lockheed selected the Rolls Royce RB211 engine to power its L-1011 Tristar wide-bodied commercial transport. Until the termination of L-1011 production in 1983, Rolls Royce remained the exclusive supplier of engines to the L-1011 program. Rolls Royce was nationalized by the British government in 1971, following bankruptcy resulting from expenses incurred in the development of the RB211. In 1973, Rolls Royce achieved a position on the Boeing 747 with an uprated version of the RB211, and thus placed itself in direct competition with Pratt and Whitney and General Electric. Rolls Royce has been unsuccessful to date in achieving a position on the Airbus Industrie's A300 and A310 airplanes, while both U.S. manufacturers supply engines for these aircraft.

Figure 5-7 indicates that the Rolls Royce RB211 engine family has near parity in terms of thrust and specific fuel consumption against the two U.S. manufacturers. However, as shown in Figures 5-7 and 5-8, Rolls Royce has lagged behind Pratt and Whitney and General Electric in thrust-to-weight ratio and turbine temperature.

Thrust growth within an engine family is usually achieved by increasing turbine temperature, and the deficiencies of Rolls Royce in high turbine temperature technology placed it at a competitive disadvantage especially during the early 1970s.

Rolls Royce has acted to bring its turbine temperature technology up to the state of the art of the two U.S. engine manufacturers. In 1968 Rolls Royce established a High Temperature Demonstrator Unit (HTDU) and an associated ongoing research and development effort. Rolls Royce is seeking to extend its technology in the areas of turbine blade and nozzle guide vane cooling, turbine aerodynamics, and application of advanced manufacturing techniques and new materials to turbines. While Rolls Royce did not keep pace with Pratt and Whitney and General Electric through the 1970s, Figure 5-9 indicates that Rolls Royce will achieve parity in turbine temperature technologies by the mid-1980s. The length of time needed for Rolls Royce to catch up is indicative of the long lead times required for research, development, and the introduction to production of engine technological advancements. Rolls Royce recovery efforts in this area demonstrate its determination to remain a viable competitor with Pratt and Whitney and General Electric.

SNECMA Engine Technologies and Programs

SNECMA is the French manufacturer of large gas turbine air-craft engines and is 85 percent owned by the French government. The company designed, developed, and currently produces the ATAR and M53 engines powering the French Armed Forces' Mirage and Super Etendard fighter bombers. Additionally, SNECMA has a 50 percent codevelopment and production share of the CFM56 commercial transport engine family and a 10 percent codevelopment share of the CF6-80C. SNECMA's execution of its share of these programs, and earlier programs with Rolls Royce on the Olympus engine, has been up to the state-of-the-art standards of U.S. manufacturers.

SNECMA does not have a complete technology base now, particularly in high-stage-loading compressors, high-space-rate combustors, and high-temperature turbines. SNECMA and French government labs are developing such technology through R&D work on eutectic alloys and structural composites.

In general, many of the technologies incorporated in commercial transport engines are also applicable to military fighter engines; typically, there is a high degree of synergistic technology transfer between military and commercial engine designs. Thus, examination of SNECMA's fighter engine technology compared with that of Pratt and Whitney and General Electric provides some further assessment of SNECMA's technological competitiveness. Figures 5-10 and 5-11 compare two significant measures of overall technology level for fighter engines: thrust-to-weight ratio and turbine temperature. The data would indicate performance levels for the M88 below those of the latest U.S. fighter engines (F100, F404, and F110) and also lagging some 8 to 10 years in development, if needed funds are found for the program. It should be noted that the SNECMA development is proceeding without a specific application objective to pace it.

MTU Engine Technologies and Programs

The West German firm Motoren-und-Turbinen-Union GmbH (MTU) also participates as a codevelopment and coproduction partner in several large commercial transport and military engine programs. Its technical execution of the engine modules, for which it has had codevelopment responsibility, has been comparable to state-of-the-art standards of U.S. manufacturers.

The German government has concluded that the German market is not big enough to justify an independent capability in large commercial transport engines. The government has concluded that further investment for a small turboshaft develop-

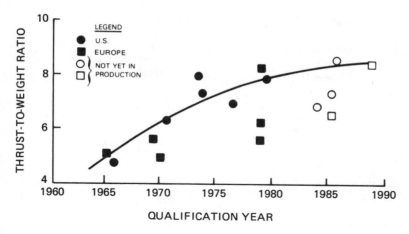

FIGURE 5-10 Military Engines--Thrust-To-Weight Ratio (manufacturer's quoted performance)

SOURCE: Pratt and Whitney, from data supplied by manufacturers.

ment might be low enough, and its market large enough, to support an MTU independent venture or majority partnership. MTU, along with Turbomeca, has been studying a joint venture engine in the 1000-shp class, the MTM 385, to power a new European helicopter.

The government does not want to expand its engine industry to handle peak loads, leaving idle capacity to be filled by makework. It will probably remain a high-technology partner with the three principal manufacturers and is likely to attempt to increase its share of participation in future commercial programs.

Volvo Flygmotor Engine Technologies and Programs

In Sweden, Volvo Flygmotor engine activities are heavily oriented toward military engines. The company has pursued a long-range strategy of expanding its civil aeroengine and nonaerospace business segments to achieve a balance in sales among military engines, commercial engines, and nonaerospace products (such as hydraulic motors). Since 1972, it has increased its civil engine share from 3 to 13 percent of sales and its nonaerospace business from 7 to 31 percent. Military engines are 56 percent of total sales. Volvo Flygmotor does not have a complete technology base, particularly for high-stage-loading compressors and high-

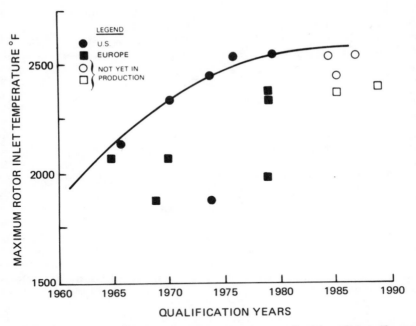

FIGURE 5-11 Military Engines--Maximum Turbine Inlet Temperature (manufacturer's quoted performance)

SOURCE: Pratt and Whitney, from data supplied by manufacturers.

temperature turbines, and it does not have good capability in fan, combustion, and afterburner/thrust reverser technology.

Swedish national policy for the last 45 years has called for self-sufficiency in the manufacture and support of military engines. This has been interpreted to include design and development of derivative models adapted to unique Swedish operating specifications. The Swedish government has funded such R&D. Volvo Flygmotor has said that its industrial competence makes it an attractive partner and that it intends to be a prime source, worldwide, for a selected range of components.[1]

Japanese Engine Industry Technologies and Programs

Three Japanese companies, Ishikawajima-Harima Heavy Industries (IHI), Mitsubishi Heavy Industries (MHI), and Kawasaki Heavy Industries, (KHI), along with the government National

Aerospace Laboratory (NAL), are responsible for Japanese engine research, development, and manufacturing efforts.

MHI has been involved in licensed production of JT8D-M9 engines and also in commercial overhaul and repair of turbofan engines since about 1972. IHI, the largest of the three, is the prime contractor for F-100 engines, produced under license and used on the Japanese-built F-15 fighters.

In 1979 these three companies established a domestic consortium, Japan Aero Engines Corporation (JAEC), which joined with Rolls Royce to develop a new engine (the RJ500) for the 150-passenger airplane market. This development has evolved into the V2500 engine and been supplanted by an expanded multinational consortium in which the Japanese companies (through JAEC) participate as a 23 percent risk-sharing partner. The others include Pratt and Whitney along with Rolls Royce (each with 30 percent shares), and also MTU and Fiat (with 11 percent and 6 percent, respectively).

The most ambitious independent Japanese engine effort to date has been the FJR710. This engine, begun in 1971 under sponsorship of NAL and subcontracted to IHI, MHI, and KHI, is an 11,000-pound thrust, high bypass ratio turbofan engine. Figures 5-7 through 5-9 show that the FJR710 is not compatible with today's commercial transport engines. Development of the engine has proceeded slowly, suggesting a focus on development and demonstration rather than a viable commercial engine.

The Japanese plan to invest $181.6 million through 1986 on the V2500's development--essentially a doubling of the $93 million that has thus far been allocated to the FJR710 program. While Japan's participation in the V2500 program is that of a minority partner, its longer-term objectives in the development of contributing engine technologies--in high-temperature alloys, coatings, and ceramics--should not be overlooked.

Status of General Aviation, Regional, and Rotorcraft Propulsion

All three types of aircraft, of course, use smaller powerplants and gearboxes to transfer power. Thus, the benefits of advances in large engines do not accrue to these smaller versions. The advances in high-temperature materials technology are applicable, and the strength of the U.S. infrastructure in these materials is valuable. The U.S. is thought to be ahead in propulsion technology for all of these aircraft. As noted earlier, the Canadian government has targeted engines of this size as an opportunity and is supporting development. In doing so, Canada is able to capitalize on proximity to high-temperature materials capability in the United States.

There are currently 18 jet engine manufacturers in the free world and a total of 26 companies participating as licencees, consortia members, or joint venture partners. The three manufacturers of large engines and their associated companies account for approximately 75 percent of the market. Their share of the market for engines under 5,000 lbs. thrust, however, drops to under 45 percent. Four other U.S. companies--Garrett, Lycoming, Allison, and Williams Research--have more than 40 percent of the market.

The development cost of a new engine in this size range is from $200 million to $1 billion, and these smaller engine manufacturers are marginal with respect to their ability to fund the development of a new engine. They face a formidable task in competing with companies receiving government support. Just as in the case of smaller aircraft, the technology and capital requirements for these smaller engines are a more attainable target for smaller countries. West Germany, France, Italy, Sweden, Japan, and Israel all have active entrants in this field.

Engine Development and Production Capabilities

Commercial transport engine development and production capabilities are strongly dependent on (1) the availability of specialized test facilities such as altitude chambers and wind tunnels, (2) the manpower available in the industry, and (3) suitable production facilities.

Altitude Test Chambers and Wind Tunnels Figure 5-12 and Table 5-1 show the availability and capability of engine altitude test chambers of sufficient size to test medium- and large-sized commercial transport engines. Both the United States and the United Kingdom have test facilities available. The only other country currently possessing a suitable facility is France.

The Office of Science and Technology Policy (OSTP) report on Aeronautical Research and Technology Policy indicates that "... with minor exceptions, existing and planned [U.S.] major facilities are adequate and will not require replacement in the near future."[2] A 1981 study was conducted by NASA titled Survey of Altitude Test Facilities and Wind Tunnels--U.S.A. and Foreign. Information in this report, summarized in Figure 5-12 and Table 5-1, which lists major United States and foreign altitude chambers and wind tunnels, indicates that Europe, in general, has sufficient modern test facilities to support independent development of engines by European manufacturers.[3]

Japan lacks altitude test chambers and wind tunnels to support research and development of engines. The recent altitude test of

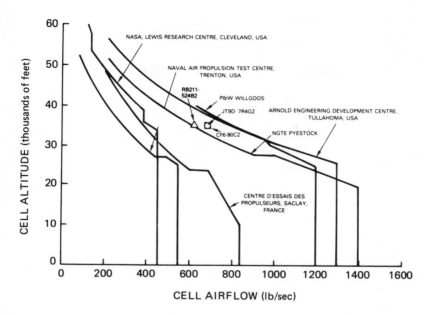

FIGURE 5-12 International Altitude Test Facilities Capability

SOURCE: Survey of Altitude Test Facilities and Wind Tunnels--
U.S. and Foreign; NASA.

the FJR710 was accomplished in Great Britain's National Gas
Turbine Establishment. The report <u>Aeronautical Research and
Technology Policy</u> states, "Japan lacks a focal point for aeronautical research such as NASA, as well as important facilities
for aeronautical research, particularly in areas of propulsion."[4]

<u>Manpower</u> Table 5-2 compares the manpower employed by the
companies building commercial transport engines or their major
components in 1979, which was a good employment year for the
industry. A comparison based on 1982-1983 employment would be
misleading due to the current distressed condition of the commercial transport aircraft segment of the aerospace industry.
   In the future, Japan can be expected to increase its staffing in
the aerospace industry. The white collar segment of Japan's
working population is heavily weighted toward engineers and
scientists compared with the U.S., and its educational system

TABLE 5-1 Subsonic and Transonic Wind Tunnel Facilities

Country	Facility	Dimensions (in feet)	Mach Number Capability	Remarks
France (C.E. Pr.)	S2-MA	6.3 × 5.75	0.1	
	F-1	14.8 × 11.5	0.0-0.36	High-lift devices
	S1-MA	20.5 × 22	0.02-1.0	Aerodynamic and engine
England	RAE 5M	16 × 14	0.0-0.33	High-lift devices
	RAE	8 × 8	0.1-0.85	
	RAE	24 Dia.	0.0-0.15	Noise
	ARA	9 × 8	0.3-1.4	
Netherlands	NLR	7 × 10	0.0-0.2	
	NLR	6.8 × 5.4	0.2-1.4	
	DNW	26.5 × 20	0.0-0.3	Aerodynamic and engine
		31.0 × 31.0	0.0-0.18	
		20 × 20	0.0-0.43	
Canada	NAE LST	6 × 9	0.0-0.27	
Switzerland	EFW	23.1 Dia.	0.0-0.24	
	EFW	26.4 × 18.8	0.0-0.15	
United States	LERC	6 × 9	0.0-0.4	Icing
		9 × 15	0.0-0.2	Noise
		10 × 10	0.0-0.4	Propulsion
		8 × 6	0.4-2.0	Propulsion
	ARC	40 × 80	0.0-0.4	Propulsion
		80 × 120	0.0-0.1	Propulsion
		12 Dia.	0.0-0.1	
		14 Dia.	0.6-1.2	
		11 × 11	0.4-1.4	
		6 × 6	0.2-2.2	
	LRC	30 × 60	0.0-0.1	Propulsion
		7 × 7	0.2-1.3	
		16 Dia.	0.2-1.3	
		16 × 16	0.0-1.2	

SOURCE: Survey of Altitude Test Facilities and Wind Tunnels—U.S. and Foreign; NASA.

TABLE 5-2 1979 Engine Division Employment

Companies	Employees
U.S.	
Pratt and Whitney	43,800
General Electric	30,000
Foreign	
Rolls Royce	52,200
SNECMA	18,400
MTU	6,000
FIAT Aviazione	2,700
Volvo Flygmotor	3,000*
IHI	4,000
Mitsubishi	500
Kawasaki	1,200

*1978 data (1979 not available.

SOURCE: Pratt and Whitney, General Electric, Flight International.

supports this emphasis. As an example, out of every 10,000 citizens in the United States, 20 are lawyers, 40 are accountants, and 70 are engineers and scientists. In Japan, there are 1 lawyer, 3 accountants, and 400 engineers and scientists per 10,000 population.

International Joint Ventures to Develop and Produce Commercial Transport Aircraft Engines The General Electric-SNECMA codevelopment agreement on the CFM56 was established in the early 1970s. Since then, joint-venture partnerships between an American engine manufacturer and European and Japanese manufacturers have become an established approach for new commercial transport engine programs. The following large commercial transport engine codevelopment and coproduction agreements are currently in place or are proposed:

1. General Electric/SNECMA   CFM56
2. GE/SNECMA/MTU   CF6-50
3. GE/SNECMA/MTU/Volvo Flygmotor   CF6-80
4. Pratt & Whitney/MTU/Fiat   PW2037
5. Pratt & Whitney/MTU/Fiat/
   Rolls Royce/IHI/MHI/KHI   *V2500
   *International Aero Engines, Inc.

Recently, Pratt & Whitney and General Electric have been studying advanced turbofan engines with technology beyond that of the NASA-sponsored Energy Efficient Engine (E^3) demonstrators. These studies have identified further potential for improving fuel consumption of about 12 percent, which could be available after the year 2000. Additionally, the propfan concept, mentioned earlier, utilizing a thin-bladed propeller of advanced design to operate efficiently at flight speeds approaching those of turbofan-powered airplanes, holds promise of reducing fuel consumption by up to 30 to 35 percent compared with today's turbofans. The appreciable potential gains available from propulsion systems make it reasonable to assume that new commercial engine program opportunities will emerge.

With international joint ventures likely for future commercial transport engine development programs, it is important that U.S. engine manufacturers maintain their current technical leadership and thus retain the lead role in future development programs. The maintenance of technical leadership and the retention of market shares large enough to support the production base of the U.S. engine industry will be challenging in the face of development and production subsidies extended by foreign governments to their manufacturers.

Within the powerplant segment of the aeronautics industry, the U.S. has gained competitive advantage not only from its accumulated massive civil transport development and experience, but from advances in system design and performance sponsored by DOD. It would appear that powerplants could be built by the mid-1990s with approximately 10 percent better thrust-to-weight ratios and 15 to 20 percent lower specific fuel consumption than the "energy efficient engine" technology that evolved from recent NASA activity. The market push, because of dollar volume, is stronger for large-aircraft powerplant development than for small. Similar technology achievements are feasible and are being pursued, but to a lesser degree for small powerplants. Foreign competition is very active in the small engine area.

Inherent in the system synthesis for advanced aircraft designs is industry's ability to produce and apply complex avionics systems that can provide more effective operating functions at lower power consumption and overall weights. Here, too, military developments help by stringent requirements for ultrareliable, fault-tolerant system design and the support of a production base that keeps costs lower.

MAINTAINING MOMENTUM
IN RESEARCH AND DEVELOPMENT

A series of mutually reinforcing factors has enabled the United States to maintain the degree of competitive and commercial leadership in civil aircraft that it has at present. The bedrock of that leadership is technology--its effective use provides superior performance and economy at competitive prices. Given the significant opportunities for further technological progress that have been identified, it is apparent that maintaining momentum in R&D is critical for preserving technological leadership. Important technological advances are not yet fully validated, and their embodiment in new aircraft, in many cases, will not occur until the 1990s. This long delay between technology development and its incorporation into new products creates vulnerability, because loss of momentum in R&D would not be apparent in the deterioration of competitive position in the U.S.--probably until it was firmly entrenched.

The growing trend toward internationalization of aircraft manufacture, with its inevitable sharing of technology with foreign partners, lends even greater urgency to the need to insure the vitality of our basic research and technology development effort. Although some information is undoubtedly transferred in international joint ventures for manufacture, the technical knowledge underlying the embodiment need not be. The technical leadership of the United States as a development partner need not be threatened provided that the United States maintains a vigorous program of basic research and technology development.

Role of NASA

The National Aeronautics and Space Administration (NASA) is the focal agency for government support of aeronautical technology. The act creating NASA charged it with "preserving the role of the United States as a leader in aeronautical science and technology...."[5] Its responsibilities covered both civil and military applications. NASA replaced the National Advisory Committee for Aeronautics (NACA), established in 1915 to "guide and supervise the fledgling science of aeronautics in practical military and civil applications."[6] NASA made significant diversions of "aeronautical capabilities and managerial attention to space activities,"[7] because it had been created to guide the U.S. space program. Figure 5-13 shows the decline in manpower devoted to aeronautical technology after the creation of NASA.

In view of the high cost of aeronautical R&D and the massive facilities required to conduct experimental programs, no other organization--and certainly no private enterprise--can perform the central role in the development of new technology that NASA carries out.

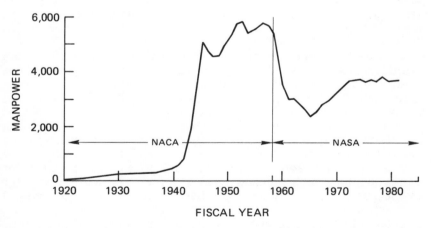

FIGURE 5-13 NACA/NASA Aeronautics Manpower History

SOURCE: NASA's Role in Aeronautics: A Workshop, Volume I Summary, p. 41, National Academy Press, Washington, DC, 1981.

There is little doubt that budget priorities reflect perceived political appeal and that space programs have been deemed to be more important than aeronautics. However, it is important for budget priorities also to reflect technological and economic opportunities and the altered competitive context that has been described in this study. Thus, the status of the international competition needs to be fully appreciated before making judgments on priorities. Examination of European and Japanese investments of public funds in R&D does not provide a clear picture of their activity. Their accounting and public reporting practices do not provide the information needed to separate the R&D funds related to generic work from funds allocated for the development and production of aircraft and engines. Thus, it is difficult to compare directly the funds of the United States devoted to R&D with those of other nations. It is likely, however, that expenditures by others for generic R&D are, in the aggregate, approximately equal to those in the United States. The technical accomplishments of the Concorde supersonic transport, Airbus A300, A310, RB-211 turbofan engine, RJ-500 turbofan engine, ATR 42 commuter transport, and helicopters suggest a sound preceding research and development program.

The panel recommends reexamination of the research and technology development activity in support of civil aviation in NASA in the light of the changing competitive environment and the technical opportunities noted in this study.

As can be seen in Table 5-3, aeronautical R&D represents approximately 5 percent of total R&D. Considering the importance of civil aircraft manufacture to economic health, societal good, and the balance of payments, there would seem to be reason to reexamine priorities and levels of expenditures. The NRC study, cited above, concluded that the problem did not result from the dual responsibility of NASA for space and for aviation. As has been noted, the need is to rethink the importance of advancing aeronautical technology to the American public and to national goals of economic strength and strategic security in the light of the changed competitive environment.

Another development need also warrants attention. The present institutional mechanisms for developing and applying new technology do not address adequately the investment required for validating new technological advances for certification and for public acceptance. In the classical sequence of R&D new physical principles, configurations, structures, etc. are conceived and evaluated in the research and technology phase through analytical modeling, simulation, and flight research techniques as appropriate. For the technology to be ready for application its inherent risk factors must be fully understood by working with systems

TABLE 5-3   NASA Budget Authority, 1968-1983
(millions of dollars)

Year	Total	R&D	Aeronautical R&T
1968	4,589	3,912	NA
1969	3,995	3,314	NA
1970	3,749	2,993	96
1971	3,312	2,556	102
1972	3,308	2,523	109
1973	3,408	2,599	157
1974	3,040	2,194	168
1975	3,231	2,323	167
1976	3,552	2,678	175
1977	3,819	2,856	190
1978	4,064	3,012	228
1979	4,559	3,477	264
1980	5,243	4,088	308
1981	5,522	4,334	271
1982	6,020	4,772	265
1983	6,839	5,543	280

SOURCE: Aerospace Industries Association of America, Inc., *Aerospace Facts and Figures*, 1983/1984, pp. 74 and 76.

that approximate full scale under representative flight or other simulated operating conditions. In this process (called validation) the component subsystem or system technology to be validated is generic, not specific to a design under development--not a prototype or actual product development. This validation stage provides the expanded knowledge necessary for enabling designers to incorporate the new advance into a specific product with a high degree of confidence in its performance and in the integrity and certificability of the product.

There is no way that validation can be satisfactorily circumvented. It is the longest and most expensive part in the chain of advancing new technology. (It has also at this point where the momentum of the United States' R&D has become most vulnerable.) Industrial firms lack the resources to undertake expensive, long-term, and uncertain work of this nature; they have no public franchise that would legitimize their undertaking it; and no standards have been established to satisfy public opinion in an area where questions of safety are central. NASA has traditionally carried out the early phases of basic and applied research, while aircraft manufacturers have assumed responsibility for incorporating new technology into designs and obtaining certification. In the past the armed forces have played an important role in some validation, e.g., turbine engines, sweptback wings, and supersonic flight, but the generic technology supported by DOD has been significantly curtailed over the past 15 years.

The technology validation phase is within NASA's charter, but here also, it has received limited funding and support. The panel believes that the national implications of this gap in technology development have not been fully understood.

The panel recommends reconsideration of NASA's activities and the resources available to support technology validation.

An additional area in which NASA is not now active involves the flight, demonstration of long life, and basic process under-standing of composites. Composites play a special role in future performance gains for aircraft. In addition to reductions in manu-facturing cost that must be achieved by individual producers, their extended use will require significant advances in process automation, in nondestructive testing and inspection, in devel-oping standard strength-of-materials data for use by designers, in evaluation of operational life and suitability, and in establishing design criteria for crash-worthiness. If these new materials are to be used in primary structures, it will be necessary to insure their integrity not only at installation but also during use. This means that progress in material processing and test techniques is as important as progress on composites themselves. An endeavor of this sort would clearly benefit from joint NASA-DOD-industry planning and participation. Consequently, an expanded role for NASA might also include accelerated service testing and work on evaluation technologies as part of the validation of new materials for use in primary structures.

An expansion of NASA's activities into technology validation and evaluation of composite materials should include mechanisms to insure that areas selected for additional effort are relevant to the needs of industry and that the results will be of such a nature that they can be applied with confidence. One possible mech-anism for ensuring relevance involves joint industry-government program definition. Another mechanism could be through aug-mentation of the present NASA aeronautics advisory committee structure. Similar committees have been effective in the past. The advisors included representatives from industry, universities, the airlines and from other involved government agencies, especi-ally the DOD and FAA. The Aeronautics and Space Engineering Board of the National Research Council could make a contribu-tion, as could the Aeronautics Committee of the NASA Advisory Council. The newly established OSTP Aeronautical Policy Review Commmittee can play a special role in such process because it reports to the President through the science advisor.

The OSTP study of aeronautical R&D policy noted that both the Soviet Union and our commercial competitors actively collect, read, and evaluate published U.S. aeronautical technical data, which are widely distributed. The panel recognizes the value of trying to extract maximum domestic value from technical information generated by public funds. Attempts to impose restrictions--however laudible their intent--must be sensitive to a long history of unfortunate consequences of similar past efforts. Any new effort to reexamine this problem will need to recognize the value of international technical cooperation and research exchanges at the university level.

The growing technological strength of foreign competitors is creating a considerable amount of foreign-based aeronautical R&D in the technical literature. NASA does not collect and evaluate the best foreign R&D and distribute reviews or assessments to the U.S. technical community. In general, U.S. industry also has not been aggressive in monitoring and applying foreign technical advances.

The panel concurs in the OSTP recommendation that NASA collect and evaluate foreign R&D and distribute results to the U.S. technical community. The panel also recommends that U.S. aircraft manufacturers and firms in the supporting infrastructure assign higher priority to the collection and evaluation of foreign technology and build their capability to do so.

Role of FAA

The FAA is responsible for flight safety, operational safety, and certification of new aircraft, equipment, and procedures. Through coordination with NASA in formulating the rules for certification, the FAA can help accelerate the development of the technology base, its application and certification, and its acceptance by designers, developers, and buyers. Special attention should be devoted to the rapid advances in electronics and their use for flight control, for air traffic control, and for general operations. If this is done in concert with NASA's technology development, it will shorten the time for certification and for the introduction of such advances in aircraft and operational systems by manufacturers. The industrial members of the panel believe that more effective coupling between NASA and FAA as technology development proceeds would reduce uncertainty for aircraft designers in obtaining certification of new aircraft.

The panel recommends that the FAA work closely with NASA in the definition and implementation of validation programs to include those aspects of technology pertinent to FAA's mission responsibilities--flight safety, operational safety, and related certification.

NOTES

1. Flight-International, January 8, 1983, pg. 67.
2. Aeronautical Research and Technology Policy, Volume II: Final Report, Office of Science and Technology Policy, November 1982, p. II-44.
3. NASA's Role in Aeronautics: A Workshop, Volume 1 Summary, Appendix A, p. 37, National Academy Press, Washington, D.C., 1981.
4. Aeronautical Research and Technology Policy, Volume II: Final Report, Office of Science and Technology Policy, November 1982, p. II-44.
5. NASA's Role in Aeronautics: A Workshop, Volume 1 Summary, Appendix A, p. 37, National Academy Press, Washington, D.C., 1981.
6. Ibid.
7. Ibid.

6
Key Policy Issues

In considering the likely competitive future of U.S. civil air-craft manufacture, one must examine separately the major elements of the industry: large transports, helicopters, and general aviation--including commuters, executive aircraft, and light air-craft. In large transports the U.S. position of dominance has been shaken but remains strong. The future environment will be different, however, and could be characterized as competitive international interdependence. Given the close tie between civil aviation and national security, it is in the national security interests of the United States to have a viable civil aviation industry--including both airlines and aircraft manufacture. If the United States were to end up with only one large air transport manufacturer (a scenario that is not too improbable) our long commitment to efficiency through competition would no doubt lead us to wish an alternative supply from some source.

The challenge within the United States is to preserve the strength and effectiveness of the large transport industry as it accommodates to higher financial risks, increased competition, the need to assure access to foreign markets, and increased market uncertainty.

The environment for the other categories of aircraft is different in character and scale. The smaller size and lower capital requirements to develop these aircraft and their powerplants make them a more suitable vehicle for many nations to enter the civil aircraft market. Since deregulation the U.S. market for commuter aircraft has been perceived as being much larger than in the past. U.S. manufacturers are now beginning to address these opportunities, but they are tardy compared with many foreign entries. Furthermore, they will find it necessary to penetrate world markets if they expect to achieve needed economies of scale. U.S. manufacturers do not start from a position of dominance in the market for smaller transport aircraft. However, when considering policy alternatives and priorities one cannot

141

invoke the argument for national security with the same force that applies to large transports.

Helicopters represent a special area of technology. Their importance to national security is clear. The growing success of foreign competitors, which is based partly on U.S. technology, is also clear. It would appear that foreign nations have been more adroit at stabilizing military procurement and phasing it with civilian sales. In the United States, military helicopter development has diverged from dual-use concepts, and although the state of the art has been maintained, the cost of commercial development has increased. Attainment of dual-use capability warrants reexamination for military helicopters that are designed for transport use.

This study has identified six key policy issues to which attention should be given by government, industry, and organized labor.

TRADE POLICY

International competition in aircraft production has crossed a watershed; it has moved from being almost a contradiction in terms to something of major concern. As this study has noted, the U.S. aircraft industry is now often in virtual competition with governments, not just with private commercial enterprises. Foreign governments are deeply involved in the financing of design, development, production, marketing, and sale of aircraft. They assume some or all of the financial, technological, and market risk associated with these endeavors. In parallel, they exert political pressures during the purchase of aircraft by their own and other airlines. Furthermore, they do not necessarily judge success or failure by the normal commercial standards of market acceptance and return on investment that apply to the U.S. private sector. Their criteria include national prestige, creation of an indigenous technology and production base, provision of employment and training of the work force, substitution for imports, evolution from a low-technology to a high-technology economy, and preservation of foreign currency. These directed efforts apply to commuter aircraft, helicopters, and business jets as well as to large commercial transports and their engines and components.

The increased competitive strength of foreign manufacturers is appearing at a time of declining U.S. dominance and leadership in world markets and is fostering disturbing U.S. pressures to increase protectionism. In the coming decade 60 percent or more of the world aircraft market for large civil transports will be outside the United States. These export markets were previously dominated by U.S. manufacturers. This fact alone supports the conclusion that pursuing an effective U.S. trade policy to permit U.S. manufacturers to enter and compete on a fair basis is essential.

Developing countries represent one of the major growth markets for aircraft. The general trend of increasing the barriers for exports from developing countries to the United States and other industrialized nations may result reciprocally in a severe impact on U.S. aircraft exports to these markets. The ability of developing countries to import is critically dependent on their ability to finance the purchases with exports. Otherwise they cannot generate the foreign currency to purchase aircraft and other goods and services. This increases the importance of trade for the developing countries and demonstrates the significance of financing as a competitive weapon. Thus, there is the need to increase the priority for a well-articulated, comprehensive, timely foreign trade policy toward developing as well as developed nations.

U.S. international trade policy in high-technology industries is being forced to focus on a new set of issues. The central issues in earlier multilateral negotiations in the postwar period, e.g., the Kennedy and Tokyo Rounds, were tariff reductions (however, Tokyo did address nontariff issues as well). Tariffs are not now the central trade policy issues in aircraft and other high-technology industries. Instead, nontariff barriers to market access--such as governmentally directed procurement--or more subtle forms of foreign government subsidy are the central issues. This new form of international competition in high-technology industries was the basis for the Agreement on Trade in Civil Aircraft that was negotiated in parallel with the final set of Tokyo Round talks. However, nontariff barriers and some forms of subsidy are far less visible and much more difficult to monitor than are tariffs, e.g., cross-trading, grants, deferred paybacks, special grants and services with no costs or below-market costs, and contingent sale of military aircraft.

The position of the United States on subsidizing higher-technology development provides competing nations with a basis for justifying their forms of subsidy. The long, productive relationship of NASA, its predecessor NACA, and the aircraft industry is one example. Similarly, historical examples of spinoff to the civilian sector from military development and procurement provide further ammunition to other nations in the negotiation over trade.

U.S. trade policy for aircraft, and other industrial products as well, has focused on defining the framework--the rules of conduct--under which both industry and governments are expected to operate. In that process, the U.S. government has had as its primary objective insuring that U.S. industry had the opportunity to compete on fair terms in the international markets.

The new impediments to trade admit of a virtually infinite variety of obstacles. Thus, continued focus of U.S. trade policy on a careful specification of the "rules of the game" is open to difficulties in today's operating environment. The high visibility of tariffs in the past meant that enforcement of trade agreements was a relatively simple undertaking. Faced with a broad and constantly changing array of foreign nontariff barriers, U.S. trade policy now must devote a much higher level of resources and attention to the monitoring and enforcement of multilateral agreements on the rules and actual practice of the game--and with a growing list of competitor nations.

The relative ease with which nontariff barriers may be altered and manipulated means that U.S. trade negotiators, and the agencies that support them, need the resources to delineate acceptable and unacceptable practices in an arena where international competitors are continually seeking ways of avoiding the restrictions of multilateral agreements in order to gain commercial advantage. This administrative support structure must also have the resources to marshal evidence regarding practices being followed. Recent steps to strengthen the resources for monitoring compliance and for discussing problems with trading partners are a hopeful signal of increased priority on trade issues. In order to insure stability and consistency it is important for the value of the work to be so broadly accepted that it will not be undone by a subsequent administration. The present staff is to be commended for its competence and commitment, but it faces a monumental task in monitoring, data gathering, and analysis. An effective trade policy must include institutional arrangements to insure that balance is achieved among differing and conflicting policy objectives, and that mechanisms exist for rationalizing and coordinating the policy balancing process.

Consideration should also be given to the development of a broader arsenal of response mechanisms, such as temporary tax, financial support, or import limitations, that would permit more carefully targeted responses. The development of greater flexibility in timeliness of responses also warrants study. This step requires greater foresight by the private sector and continuing effective relationships between the trade administration and the private sector. The rapid pace of commercial transactions can easily render an eventual response useless unless administrative action matches the pace of commerce.

The situation with respect to Eximbank policies and procedures reflects the greater ambivalence and lower priority associated with international trade in the United States. The commitments of the bank represent a potential drain on the U.S. Treasury, and in a time of huge deficits all such potentials warrant careful scrutiny. Nevertheless, competition over the terms of financing is often central in international sales of aircraft. The present ingenuity being demonstrated by both financial institutions and aircraft manufacturers in devising new financial instruments, new leasing conditions, creative use of insurance, increased use of international sources of capital, and conversion into currencies that aid repayment is to be commended and should be continued. However, the importance of Eximbank as a lender and guarantor requires that it have both the lending conditions in terms of payback period, interest charged, percent of assets covered, front-end money, etc., and the administrative practices, especially with respect to support of smaller transactions, that can match competition. In order to be effective, Eximbank needs to have available mechanisms and administrative practices that provide a credible force for achieving the basic U.S. position, which is to insure that international market rate and market terms apply equitably to all transactions. The more evident and credible the arsenal of responses available, the more likely that the market will discipline itself.

One especially troublesome aspect of financing involves competition with international suppliers for domestic sales. If the mechanisms permit it, domestic airlines will seek to stimulate below-market financing from foreign vendors to force better terms from domestic suppliers. Mechanisms and policies must be developed to uncover and counter such practices.

The development and administration of an effective trade policy requires that all involved interests be balanced to resolve policy issues facing our government. The panel supports the recent consensus expressed by the National Research Council Panel on Advanced Technology Competition and the Industrialized Allies that recommended in part that "the federal government should initiate a biennial, cabinet-level review to assess U.S. trade competitiveness..." and that this review "...should be supported by a continuing mechanism that would draw on expertise both from within the government and from outside.[1]

Beyond the restructuring of the policy process, however, the panel supports the scrutiny and political debate now beginning on the entire subject of trade policy. A more strategic approach may well be necessary for the United States to achieve both better focus and better differentiation among industrial sectors regarding their importance to international trade and the differences in competitive environment within which they operate.

In so doing, it is important to include in the deliberations an informed awareness of the balances achieved by our international commercial competitors. It is apparent that the governments of the countries in which they operate have attached greater weight to trade success than has the United States.

The subject is complex. The data concerning the effectiveness of explicit industrial policies implemented in other countries are incomplete, giving rise to varying interpretations. Any proposed changes in U.S. policy must recognize our own traditions, values, and institutions. Nevertheless, the future prospects of civil aircraft development and manufacturing for the U.S. industry lend urgency to the assessment.

International trade is important to the U.S. economy. It faces increasingly powerful international competition, and the entire apparatus of government--not just trade policy--tends to reflect the priorities and perceptions of an earlier time when our total international trade was much less significant. Furthermore, for a period after World War II the United States enjoyed an unsustainable economic and technological dominance that lulled us into a false sense of competitive superiority. What is needed, perhaps more than anything else, is a change in tone and attitude, the creation of a changed national consensus that gives the needed greater weight to international trade and strengthening of the U.S. competitive position.

BALANCING ECONOMIC AND SECURITY INTERESTS IN TECHNOLOGY TRANSFER

As this report has noted, international technology transfer has an impact on both the perception and the reality of U.S. national security. With the increasing importance accorded to technology, it offers potential leverage in diplomacy. The conventional view is that formulation of policy in this area requires balancing national security or foreign policy objectives against those of strengthening the economy and preserving the U.S. position in advanced technology. This study has emphasized that a broader view of national security should include economic strength and technological leadership.

It is important to recognize the changing position of the U.S. vis-à-vis that of international competitors and world markets. In technological competition, the United States appears still to have a lead in most of the technologies associated with aircraft design and manufacture; however, the lead is small, the rate of technical diffusion has increased, and both our European and Japanese competitors possess the necessary skills and capabilities to compete effectively with or without further technology transfer from the United States.

The international competitive equation has also changed due to factors other than technology. International markets are projected to grow more rapidly than U.S. domestic markets and thus become increasingly important. In addition, after many years of effort, serious international competition is now emerging in large transports and has become a major market factor for commuters, helicopters, and executive aircraft.

In this changed environment, an overt policy to restrain technology transfer provides little leverage and may serve to freeze U.S. companies out of markets and to stimulate the development of even more powerful technological competitors. Even with respect to national security, technology has value only in a limited time frame.

Cooperative programs between the United States and its allies for licensing and coproduction of aircraft are also an important factor in technology transfer. This subject also is complex. It is in the national security interest of the United States for its allies to have an indigenous aircraft industry, which inevitably represents a potential threat in civil markets. Memoranda of Understanding (MOU) have represented the legal vehicle for large-scale transfer of technology for military aircraft. Industrial representatives believe these MOUs should be written with more consideration of the international competitive impact they may have on domestic manufacturers of civil aircraft.

The key to effective policy formulation in this area is to insure that all parties with an important interest in the outcome have the opportunity for inputs. The mechanisms for marshaling the argument for national security and diplomacy are all within the government. The relevant inputs from the private sector are both more diffuse and more diverse, and the institutional arrangements for assembling and assessing these inputs are not now well articulated.

MAINTAINING MOMENTUM IN R&D

Although technological leadership is not of itself sufficient for success in the marketplace, the emergence of effective international competition increases its importance. The competitive assessment of the current promise of new technology in this study concluded that there were indeed important, attractive opportunities for further advances in aerodynamic design, controls, structure, and propulsion that would lead to greater fuel efficiency, lower noise, greater utility, and lower operating costs. In most of these technologies the United States still enjoys a lead. However, that lead is shrinking and competitors possess the skills and commitment to challenge its leadership in virtually every field. The likely increase, noted in this report, of cooperative international arrangements for the design and production of aircraft in order to spread risks, gain market access, and obtain capital will expand the potential for more rapid diffusion of technology. This approach appears to be advantageous for the United States, if it continues to support research consistently at an adequate level.

The development of new aeronautical technology involves long lead times, large expenditures, and massive facilities. Thus, the actions and decisions that could lead to a deterioration in the U.S. position might well be taken many years before their consequences become visible. Maintaining momentum in the effective aeronautical R&D complex that includes NASA, DOD, private industry, and to some extent, the FAA, is crucial to continued U.S. technological leadership. NASA is the linchpin in that complex. No other organization possesses the charter, public acceptance, resources, or capabilities to support such long-term, high-risk, expensive R&D.

The relative priority assigned to NASA aeronautics versus space technology is of particular concern. Aeronautical R&D has diminished since the start of the space program. This study questions whether present priorities reflect appropriately the relative strategic, economic, and social importance of aviation compared with that of space.

A second concern addresses the question of a gap in the flow from basic research to product development. NASA conducts basic and applied research and technology development in key areas of science and engineering. Private companies incorporate properly validated new technology into new aircraft. The crucial step of technology validation, including exposure of risk under flight or simulated flight conditions, represents at present a weakness in the sequence. The work is long-term, expensive, risky, and generic in character. NASA's charter recognizes its role in this phase, but it is not now being pursued in a manner to sustain national competitive advantage. The panel recommends that the entire validation process be reexamined.

ACHIEVING SYNERGY BETWEEN
NATIONAL SECURITY AND CIVIL AVIATION

This study has called attention repeatedly to the close linkage between national security and civil aviation. The skills and capabilities required for production of civil and military aircraft are, to a large extent, common. This applies not only to the more obvious assembly of completed aircraft, but more particularly to the massive infrastructure of thousands of firms that supply materials, components, parts, etc. The design and manufacture of civil aircraft challenges the assemblage of technical skills of design and production teams, and manufacture of civil aircraft helps keep such teams in a high state of readiness and shares payment of their overhead with military programs.

Conversely, of course, advances in military technology have often found use in civil aircraft. For many years the interests of military and civil procurement tended to move in parallel, and little thought or effort was required to insure continued synergy. The situation is changing. DOD is sponsoring the launching of fewer new aircraft, and its interests in pushing the state of technology have focused on high-speed combat aircraft. For its needs in support aircraft, it is continuing its practice of buying off-the-shelf technology.

Reinstituting careful consideration of dual-use requirements between military and civil applications, especially in support aircraft, could have helpful leverage for all classes of aircraft included in this study. Timing the procurement of military aircraft so as not to exacerbate the large swings in production that characterize the industry could also be helpful, but the panel recognizes the practical barriers to this goal.

MANAGING IN THE NEW ENVIRONMENT

The changes occurring in both the domestic and international environments pose some severe challenges for the management of civil aircraft development and manufacturing. As noted, historically the large air transport manufacturers have excelled at producing technically proficient aircraft that were well matched to market needs. Although it sold and serviced airplanes worldwide, the industry operated from an exceedingly powerful domestic base and faced little foreign competition in any markets. It dealt with a short list of customers whose characteristics were well known and who handled the financing of their own purchases.

In the environment that is emerging, the domestic manufacturers face potentially powerful competition, increasingly important international markets, and both domestic and foreign customers with uncertain futures and shaky financial resources.

As this study has indicated, additional technical opportunities are still present for important advances in technology. These technical advances will provide significant improvements in the economic performance of air transports. They will, however, require very large investments to bring the technology to the state of readiness necessary for incorporating it into new products.

The major consequences of these emerging trends are that the manufacturers are having to move from a position of strongly autonomous operation to one of complex interdependence.

The panel perceives four important challenges for management:

1. Developing an approach to managing the introduction of new technology that will spread the high cost and risk among partners to an extent that goes beyond the traditional contractor-subcontractor relationship.

2. Becoming participants in complex arrangements with customers, banks, other financial institutions, and insurers to develop new financial instruments and arrangements that will spread risk adequately to permit purchase of needed new aircraft.

3. Moving from a position of global preeminence to one of senior partnership with international partners--a change that will require sensitivity to new cultural and national nuances.

4. Achieving the necessary selectivity to maintain dominance in strategic technologies in a world where total dominance across the board is no longer possible--or even desirable, i.e., retaining the overall U.S. lead in a situation of complex partnership with foreign firms.

In all of these areas, U.S. manufacturers are demonstrating impressive flexibility and drive, but the necessary responses have just begun. Furthermore, the needed changes will be controversial because they will raise questions in the eyes of the public regarding loss of technology and displacement of American workers that cannot be answered definitively in advance.

The challenge for the manufacturers of the other classes of aircraft is more direct. They face the more immediate threat of international competition in both domestic and international markets, and they do not occupy the position of global dominance enjoyed by manufacturers of large transports. Furthermore, until recently they faced little in the way of competition. Consequently, they have had little exposure to the exigencies created by facing new, well-designed products in their markets.

The managements of these companies seem destined to feel severe pressure for many years. They have the advantage and challenge of retaining a domestic market that will continue to dominate in scale the world's markets. Historically, the relationship between these companies and the government has been remote--the companies saw little need to seek government help and the government was not set up to serve them anyway. That situation is changing. The government is now positioned to provide assistance on trade--on terms of sale of exports, restraints on imports by other countries, or unfair trade practices by international competitors. Less positive are the unintended or underweighted effects of government policies that tend to inhibit exports. It is important for both industry and government to develop even closer and more effective interactions on these problems.

MANAGING HUMAN RESOURCES

The large swings in employment in this industry are cause for concern. In addition to the human cost associated with such cyclical employment, the instability threatens the long-term capability of the skilled technical and production teams that have been assembled.

It is apparent that our international competitors, most of whom receive substantial government support, place a higher priority on providing stable employment than it is possible for individual U.S. aircraft manufacturers to provide.

Three problems need urgent attention:

• Retirement security--accruing pension benefits that are not tied solely to the fortunes of individual companies.
• Unemployment--seeking to ameliorate the severe periodic job loss.
• Training--allowing workers to develop new skills required by advancement in technology and to share equitably in the fruits of technology.

NOTE

1. International Competition in Advanced Technology: Decisions for America, Panel on Advanced Technology Competition and the Industrialized Allies, National Research Council, National Academy Press, 1983, pp. 5-6.

This report on the civil aviation manufacturing industry is one of seven industry-specific studies (listed below) that were conducted by the Committee on Technology and International Economic and Trade Issues. ". . . [T]hese reports constitute a praiseworthy though controversial undertaking by the National Academy of Engineering, for they go far beyond strict issues of engineering. Instead . . . they offer detailed assessments of competitive standing and, more to the point, of the extent to which that standing depends on technological mastery of one sort or another." Alan M. Kantrow, Harvard Business Review.

The Competitive Status of the U.S. Auto Industry, ISBN 0-309-03289-X, 1982, 203 pages, $13.95

The Competitive Status of the U.S. Machine Tool Industry, ISBN 0-309-03394-2, 1983, 78 pages, $5.95

The Competitive Status of the U.S. Pharmaceutical Industry, ISBN 0-309-03396-9, 1983, 102 pages, $9.50

The Competitive Status of the U.S. Fibers, Textiles, and Apparel Complex, ISBN 0-309-03395-0, 1983, 90 pages, $7.95

The Competitive Status of the U.S. Electronics Industry, ISBN 0-309-03397-7, 1984, 126 pages, $10.95

The Competitive Status of the U.S. Steel Industry, ISBN 0-309-03398-5, approx. 135 pages, $9.95 (prepublication price), available Spring 1985

Also of interest...

International Competition in Advanced Technology: Decisions for America ". . . should help mobilize Government support for the nation's slipping technological and international trade position. . . ." Leonard Silk, the New York Times. A blue-ribbon panel created by the National Academy of Sciences takes a critical look at the state of U.S. leadership in technological innovation and trade. ISBN 0-309-03379-9, 1983, 69 pages, $9.50

Technology, Trade, and the U.S. Economy, ISBN 0-309-02761-6, 1978, 169 pages, $9.75

Quantity discounts are available; please inquire for prices.

All orders and inquiries should be addressed to:

Order Department
National Academy Press
2101 Constitution Avenue, NW
Washington, DC 20418